The THIRD WORLD CENTURY

Charles Stewart Goodwin

UNIVERSITY
PRESS OF
AMERICA

Lanham • New York • London

University Press of America®, Inc.
4720 Boston Way
Lanham, Maryland 20706

3 Henrietta Street
London WC2E 8LU England

Printed in the United States of America
British Cataloging in Publication Information Available

Library of Congress Cataloging-in-Publication Data

Goodwin, Charles Stewart.
The third world century / Charles Stewart Goodwin.
p. cm.
1. World politics —1989- I. Title.
D860.G66 1994 909.82—dc20 94-11721 CIP

ISBN 0-8191-9534-0 (cloth : alk. paper)

∞™ The paper used in this publication meets the minimum requirements of American National Standard for Information Sciences—Permanence of Paper for Printed Library Materials, ANSI Z39.48–1984.

DEDICATION

This book is dedicated to those individuals who read, typed, and questioned my ideas, and to those who inspired me.

Contents

Preface

Over the last forty years commentators and analysts have used the term "First World" to refer to nations of the industrialized West, and eventually to Japan. The term "Second World" described the Soviet Union, its Eastern European satellites, and The People's Republic of China. "Third World" became a generic term that denoted the remaining mass of less developed nations which comprised the bulk of Latin America, Africa, and Asia.

The last decade has witnessed the splintering of the Second World and the elevation of the First to the prime arbiter of events. Some attributes of the Third World have elbowed their way to international importance. One example is the possession of vital resources, such as oil. As the new century dawns, I believe that the Third World will progressively assume greater significance. My ideas on this subject began to coalesce after reading the works of two scholars to whom I became exposed in the mid-1970s.

Geoffrey Barraclough wrote a series of articles for *New York Review of Books,* which appeared in 1975, 1976, and 1978, and a relevant book, *An Introduction to Contemporary History.*[1] One sentence sums up his views. "The issue today is whether the existing economic system upon which Western preponderance is based can withstand the challenge from the Third World."[2] That issue is even more germane to ask in the 1990s than it was in the 1970s.

Leftan Stavros Stavrianos wrote *The Promise of the Coming Dark Age,*[3] in which he contended that, "the basic thrust of world affairs in the late Twentieth and Twenty-First Centuries will be the fundamental restructuring of the global arrangements and relationships that have evolved since the voyages of Christopher Columbus and Vasco da Gama."[4] He envisioned the emergence of a renaissance-like period of creativity rising from the 'Dark Ages' depths of the post World War II era. Above all, Stavrianos made me realize that for those experiencing it, a so-called 'Dark Age' might not be manifestly identifiable as a particular aspect of history.

The genesis of my consideration of the Second World started at the height of the Cold War. A professor of mine at college, Richard Pipes, taught me as early as 1958 that the Soviet Union would likely fragment along the ethno-national lines so carefully preserved in the creation of its empire. The spewing forth of a myriad of new entities, and would-be entities, was accurately foreseen by Pipes as both cause and by-product of Soviet collapse.

My overall historical perspective has been greatly enriched by the work of Fernand Braudel. His *The Mediterranean and the Mediterranean World in the Age of Phillip II,*[5] and *Civilization and Capitalism 15th - 18th Century*, changed the way I view history. After years of being bombarded by concepts of waves and cycles and the impact of major figures on events, Braudel made me acknowledge two important things. First, ordinary people, the backbone of any state or culture, establish the essential historical rhythms and must be studied. Second, most historical themes have both deep-seated roots and constant, but often imperceptible, rates of change.

These concepts, reflections, and impressions simmered over the years. Meanwhile, wars designed by the First or Second Worlds to impose their will upon the Third failed to achieve their objectives in places like Vietnam, Algeria, and Afghanistan. The powerful muscle of OPEC[6] was intermittently flexed, starting in the early 1970s. The political and economic landscape was altered in the 1980s by the collapse of Leninist - Bolshevik regimes in the Soviet Union and Eastern Europe. Talk of a one superpower world (the United States) began to surface. Will the world be led into the Twenty-First Century by this superpower, and increasingly assume its capitalistic, democratic characteristics? I agree with Barraclough that this is not likely.

I also concur that we have a, "choice between a New International Economic Order and chaos indescribably worse than the world has ever experienced."[7] This choice does not herald either widespread acceptance of or supremacy for a United States type socio-economic system. Rather, it announces to me the eventual arrival of a new order inspired by the values and structures of the Third World. The real question, as I see it, is whether the chaos will arrive first and if it arrives, how persistent will it be?

The possibility that the social, political, and economic systems of the First World could closely follow the Second in a spiral towards moral and financial bankruptcy currently seems remote to most observers. And yet, that appears to me precisely what is most likely to happen. A glance at any media on any day in any Industrial World nation confirms that the First World is already experiencing its full share of unrest, insecurity, and economic pain. This is not to be a passing phenomenon. Their governmental systems are not working.

This does not mean that the Industrial World must necessarily have disarray and collapse. There are choices to be made. There are degrees of instability. After all, Rome didn't disappear in a day. But we should make no mistake. A new order is on the way. It seems clear to me that in the Twenty-First Century the world will no longer be dominated militarily, economically, and politically by the largely white, mostly Christian nations that have played such a major role in its history since the Fifteenth Century. The years ahead will increasingly display evidence of a new civilization as it comes boiling out of the turbulence of the Third World. What will this new civilization be? Will it contain the puritanical power of fundamental Islam? Will it be a Latin or Chinese blend of private enterprise and authoritarianism? Will it, follow the urgings of Václav Havel[8] and prolong the vitality of the First World by reformulating and redirecting individual values? Could it be some Leibowitzian[9] subsistence society rising from the ashes of apocalypse? Or will the new world order contain features of all four?

In this book the answers to these questions, and others, will chronicle the decline of one civilization and the rise of the next, much in the way civilizations have been rising, flourishing, and waning throughout the history of humanity.

---

1 Geoffrey Barraclough, *An Introduction to Contemporary History* (Pelican Books, 1967).

2 Geoffrey Barraclough, "Wealth and Power, the Politics of Food and Oil," *N.Y. Review of Books,* Aug. 7, 1975, p. 28.

3 Leftan Stavros Stavrianos, *The Promise of the Coming Dark Age* (W.H. Freeman & Co, New York, 1976).

4 Ibid., pp 167-8.

5 Fernand Braudel, T*he Mediterranean and the Mediterranean World in the Age of Philip II* (Harper & Row, New York, 1972).

6 The Organization of Petroleum Exporting Countries

7 Geoffrey Barraclouh, "The Struggle for the Third World," *New York Review of Books* Nov. 9, 1978.

8 As stated in "Politics and Conscience" and "The Power of the Powerless".

9 Walter M. Miller, Jr., *Canticle for Leibowitz* (J. B. Lippencott Company, Philadelphia, 1959).

Introduction

In order to evaluate the future it is necessary to explore both the significance of history and the shape of its change. Are events forever imprisoned by the precise regularity of a series of Mayanesque cycles? Is there continual, inexorable progress toward the nirvana of some Hegelian end? Does the world respond to the undulation of Kondratiev-like waves? Is history, as Tolstoy thought, "the product of millions of decisions by unknown men who are blind to what they are doing?"[1]

My conception is that, while all of these elements are preset to a degree, visualizing our own historical continuum from the vantage point of some fourth dimensional aerie will reveal it as an endless, patterned fabric flowing from a giant loom. The several threads of the pattern could be traced back to the beginning, although they would continually vary their widths and interaction. While each combination would contain the same basic components, the pattern changes would illustrate the intensities of the main historical themes at different times. The familiarity of the past emphasizes its perpetual importance, but it is never exactly repeated. Change is constant, the rate varying from the barely perceptible to the relatively rapid. Nothing is pre-ordained. Millions of choices determine every design. Each era has its own distinctive pattern and velocity. As we approach the threshold of the Twenty-First Century, the speed of change is accelerating, and the pattern is bearing less resemblance to its immediate predecessors.

Jose Ortega y Gasset wrote that, "people believe modern technology is more firmly established in history than all previous technologies because of its scientific foundation. But this alleged security is illusory and the unquestionable superiority of modern technology as technology even implies an element of weakness. Since it is based on the exactness of science it is dependent on mere presuppositions and conditions. . . Indeed, it is just this feeling of security which is endangering Western Civilization."[2] The initial fissures of this inherent fragility can be seen in many areas, they include: the state of the world's environment, the pressures on urban lifestyles, and profligate resource management. We must face the possibility that, "the accomplishments of American science and technology, and the conveniences they have produced, cannot compensate for the myriad of difficulties they have inflicted."[3] If Braudel is correct that, "technology is perhaps the body rather than the soul of a civilization,"[4] it increasingly seems that the developed nations of our world have a weightlifter's body with the soul of a robot. These developed nations, with the United States in the vanguard, have the optimistic arrogance to believe they can settle anywhere, control any environment, cure any disease, and overcome any obstacle. This attitude is beginning to haunt them. Challenges are proving both wider in scope and more complex in nature than initially suspected. The environment is not under control, it is rebelling. Incurable diseases are surfacing with astonishing virulence. We are caught in a vortex over which we have progressively less mastery, with progressively less financial, moral, and natural resources at our command, and it threatens to suck the life from our civilization..

Christopher Lasch pointed out that the modern idea of 'progress' is relatively recent, only starting to infuse the Industrial World in the Eighteenth Century. Our enslavement to the twin masters of growth and technology began as we realized that creating, "insatiable appetites, formerly condemned as a source of social instability and personal unhappiness, could drive the economic machine...and thus ensure a never-ending expansion of productive forces."[5] This addiction, for it is nothing less, has separated us from the respect for and the union with the forces of nature that have characterized many socio-economic systems of the past. Some remnants of this respect and union can be found scattered about the world today, and are more likely to be the harbingers of the future than the sputtering technology-driven engine.

George Kennan identified the First World's moral dilemma. "We are faced with the task of defending a high standard of living and all the luxuries of a permissive society against the jealousies...of countless millions who are just awakening to an awareness of world affairs, and who would witness without much pity or regret the disappearance of much that we value..."[6] Many perceptive individuals in the Industrial World have recognized this conundrum. Former U.S. Secretary of State, George Schultz, commented that, "The United States cannot be prosperous if two-thirds of the world is in abject misery and poverty. This country cannot be safe and at peace if two-thirds of the world is in turmoil." This scattered awareness cannot compensate for the fact that our country and its First World companions seem increasingly unable both to feed their progress-bloated life style addiction and alleviate the suffering of the world's disadvantaged. The plight of the disadvantaged, both within and without our developed societies, is a mighty call on already overburdened physical and emotional reserves. If, as Mahatma Gandhi proclaimed, "poverty is the worst form of violence," the First World is surely being repaid in kind as strife has erupted in every direction.

It would seem that the 1990s should be the coronation of the First World's triumph. But, instead of ruling, First World nations are finding themselves alone and without landmarks in an increasingly treacherous sea. Communal co-existence is a forgotten art, especially in cities choked with poverty, crime and smog. Religion is a pale imitation of the faith that has sustained past civilizations. Imagination, veneration of ancestors and a sense of unity with the past have all been swallowed by quests for personal liberation, worship of newness and reliance on technology. The soul of our society has shrunk to the vanishing point.

Many vital signs necessary for a vibrant civilization still beat strongly in the Third World and Third World segments of First World nations. I contend that it is on the foundation of such values that the cathedral of the Twenty-First Century will eventually be built. It promises then to rapidly evolve into an exciting time, this Third World Century. But it also promises to be a world very different from the one we Westerners have been accustomed to inhabit.

The lessons of history are important. Deciphering and interpreting them is often difficult and open to debate. If anything, the task is more difficult than ever today, but ignoring these lessons or believing they can be overcome has been characteristic of modern policy-makers. The recent Vietnam and Afghan Wars are but two examples of adverse outcomes from this trait. One objective of this book is an effort to unravel the skeins of the past and use them to assist in understanding the patterns of the future.

How do I define a civilization? There is neither a precise nor a generally accepted answer.

The Oxford Universal Dictionary defines civilization as the act or process of civilizing or being civilized. Fernand Braudel, categorizing the world in 1500 A.D., finds thirteen civilizations, "relatively dense populations possessing multiple assets and advantages: domestic animals, swing-ploughs, ploughs, carts, and above all, towns."[7] Kenneth Clark defined it in his book made from the television series *Civilization*. "What is Civilization? I don't know, I can't define it in abstract terms - yet. But I think I can recognize it when I see it...

However complex and solid it seems, it is actually quite fragile. It can be destroyed... Civilization means something more than energy and will and creative power... Well, very shortly, a sense of permanence... Civilized man, it seems to me, must feel that he belongs somewhere in space and time; that he consciously looks forward and back."[8]

My definition is closer to Clark's. I don't believe history has evidence of thirteen civilizations co-existing at any one time. The maximum figure I believe is two or three. But definition in this case is subjective. It is probable that the definition I use may not always coincide with others when looking at a particular entity. Generally, whether a civilization actually has been attained or not in someone's mind is less important than the evolutionary process itself, and the rhythm of rise and fall. I do basically agree with Samuel P. Huntington. "A civilization is the highest cultural grouping of people and the broadest level of cultural identity people have short of that which distinguishes humans from other species."[9]

Bound by this broad definition, I have employed the following terms virtually interchangeably: Western Civilization; Modern Civilization; First World; Industrial World, and industrial/technological nations. Realizing the borders are often ill-defined and welcome inclusion, I have chosen to regard these phrases as all being under the same umbrella. While this, from time to time, may be slightly confusing, I believe it is also accurate.

It has often been true that civilizations in their declining phases have been relatively pleasant places to live. They permit maximization of individuality, exposure to culture, and enjoyment of sybaritic pastimes. They also are likely to have weak or ineffective government. Rising civilizations, while charged with energy, can be relatively restrictive. Religion usually is a strong and controlling facet of everyday life. Social behavior is structured and circumscribed. Government functions effectively, but is usually authoritarian. Expansion consumes both individual and social vigor leaving less room for leisure and culture. A good example of such a society in our world today is the several tentacles of Fundamental Islam.

Finally, we have to recognize that despite efforts to abolish it, war on a large scale has been a feature of every century in history. The coming one is not likely to be any different. This time the seat of the conflict will probably be in Asia, particularly East Asia, where rising military and economic powers struggle for hegemony and survival. This new century, then, may well commence in the smoke and flames of battle. In all probability, it will be only as this turmoil starts to subside that the new civilizations' flowering will begin in earnest.

---

1 Paul Johnson, *Intellectuals* (Harper & Row, New York, 1988) p.1292.
2 Jose Ortega y Gasset, *History as a System* (Norton, New York, 1962) p. 73.
3 David Myers, *George Kennan and the Dilemmas of U.S. Foreign Policy* (Oxford Press, New York, 1988) p. 320.
4 Fernand Braudel, "The Perspective of the World, Vol. 3" *Civilization and Capitalism 15th - 18th Century* (Harper & Row, New York, 1984) p.68.
5 Christopher Lasch, "The True and Only Heaven: Progress and Its Critics," (W.W. Norton, New York, 1991) p.52.
6 George Kennan, *Russia, The Atom and the World* Harper & Brothers, New York, 1957) p.112.
7 Fernand Braudel, "The Structures of Everyday Life- Vol. 1," *Civilization and Capitalism 15th - 18th Century* (Harper & Row Publishers, New York, 1979) p. 57.
8 Kenneth Clark, *Civilization* (Harper Perennial, 1969) pp 1, 3, 14, & 17.
9 Samueal P. Huntington, "The Clash of Civilizations," *Foreign Affairs* 72, No. 3 (Summer 1993) p.24.

PART I

The Post World War II Order Crumbles

"All the tumult and seeming chaos, when viewed in the light of historical perspective, can be seen to represent not only the death agonies of an old order, but also the birth pangs of a new epoch - a new golden age which assuredly will outshine those of the past."

L.S. Stavrianos
The Promise of the Coming Dark Age
W.H. Freeman & Co., NY, 1976

Disintegration of the Second World

The Soviet Empire has evaporated leaving in its place a filmy coalition called the Commonwealth of Independent States (CIS) constructed around Russia, plus an explosion of national and ethnic entities. The other major Second World tenant, The People's Republic of China (PRC), is currently flourishing under a system of authoritarianism and partially free markets.

For the moment these two nations seem headed in opposite directions. At various times history has witnessed each as major powers, and has also endured their many clashes. Together they control a third of our earth's landmass and almost a fourth of its people. While the Second World is an entity no more, its prospects are vital to the rest of humanity. Its former occupants have the potential either to assist mankind to new levels of prosperity, or to plunge it into life-threatening conflict. The threads of the past contain important clues to the patterns of the future and they will be inspected.

Will Russia turn characteristically militant and expansionist? Will it, for the first time, experience flourishing democracy and free markets? Will the history of its economic weakness be reversed?

How about China? Can it resist the historical tendency to fragment? Can it restrain military power and ambition? Will the ideas of Greater China and Chinese superiority sit better with neighboring states than they have in the Past?

Clues to these answers, as well as other trends, can be read from the patterns of history.

CHAPTER 1

Russia: Past and Prognosis

Russia has virtually no history of democratic government or industrial entrepreneurship. It has traditionally been inward turning and eastward facing. It has always had a major military component to the state, but never at its head. Great Russian national fervor has usually led to Imperial control as well as aggression. All these elements have been central to Russian nationhood. They will continue to be.

THE TSARS:

In the year 987 descendants of the Vikings, intermingled with Slavs, who had built a state called Kievan Rus (successor to an earlier Viking-Slavic center around Novgorod) created the beginnings of the modern Russian nation. The warrior class, at the behest of their ruler, Prince Vladimir, adopted Christianity. After a few years Vladimir fortified his state's powerful position astride the Baltic-Black Sea trade routes when he married the daughter of the Orthodox Christian Byzantine Emperor.

Several centuries later the effective center of Rus was re-established in the North. In 1480 Ivan III, Grand Duke of Moscow, defied his Mongol overlords who had dominated the area for almost 200 years. With that act Moscow became the nexus of Orthodox Christian power in Northern Europe. As William Wallace[1] has pointed out, the Grand Duchy also sat athwart the religious and cultural divide as the eastern boundary of Western Christianity skirted the Baltic states and divided the Ukraine. As such it became the bridge to the modern, complex Russian state. Ivan IIIs grandson, Ivan IV (the Terrible), who ruled from 1539 to 1584, consolidated power in the greatly expanded Duchy, pushed its territorial reach both east and south opening the routes to Siberia and Central Asia, and became the first de facto Tsar. He also married, as his first wife, Anistasia Romanova, whose great-nephew, Michael, ascended the throne in 1619, beginning the dynasty which was to endure until the revolutions of 1917.

Another strong ruler, Peter I (The Great), became Tsar one hundred and fifty years after Ivan the Terrible. During his reign which lasted from 1692 to 1725 he exposed the closed Russian Society to Western culture and technology, curbed the power of the nobility, defeated (in 1709) the principal Northern military power, Sweden, and established his capital at St. Petersburg on the shores of the Baltic, where it was to remain until the arrival of the Bolsheviks and the Soviet Union.

Only thirty-five years after Peter's death an obscure German princess named Sophia who had married his grandson assumed the throne and ruled (from 1762-1796) as Catherine II (The Great). She reorganized the government along German lines, patronized French philosophers, annexed the Crimea (founding Odessa), colonized Alaska and exercised dominion over nations as far flung as Poland and Turkey.

Four years after Catherine II's death her grandson became Alexander I. His reign from 1801 to 1825 was marked by the dramatic repulse of Western Europe's few incursions, and Napoleon's massive invasion of 1812. Alexander's son and successor, Nicholas I (1825-1855) turned Russia's focus firmly towards Asia. At the end of his reign, allied with Turkey, he fought the Crimean War (1854-1856) against France and Britain. Alexander II, his son, had a notable rule from 1855 -1881. During that period Russia conquered the Caucasus, annexed the Central Asian territories surrounding the storied cities of Bokhara, Tashkent and Samarkand, fought a war that humbled Turkey, embraced Pan-Slavism and widened its foothold along the Northern Pacific. Alexander II also emancipated the serfs (in 1861) and was ultimately assassinated by a radical pre-socialist terrorist group. His son, the physically powerful Alexander III, ruled from 1881 to 1894. He began the process of industrialization by setting up a sophisticated metallurgical industry (still one of Russia's few industrial strong points). This created the foundation for the one period of its history (1893-1904) when Russia's economic growth outstripped both the United States and Europe.

The caretaker of this final Imperial period was Alexander's woefully unqualified younger son who governed as Tsar Nicholas II from 1894 to 1917. He fought two disastrous wars: the Russo-Japanese in 1904-5 and World War I from 1914-1917. These wars not only bled Russia's manpower (20 million died in World War I) and resources, they led to a series of destabilizing revolutions. The first was in 1904-5 (for which Lenin's older brother was executed) and the others came in 1917, finally bringing a weakened Tsardom to its knees.

Throughout the Tsarist period several characteristics, which were to recur repeatedly, became established. Power was centralized in the absolute authority of the ruler. Dissent was not permitted and repression abounded. The country was considered the personal property of the Tsar and his ruling elite. Invasions from Europe were ultimately and decisively repelled. Although the culture of the nobility was pre-occupied with Europe, the major geographical thrust was towards Asia. While most Russian peasants spoke Slavonic, the nobles spoke French, the language of government. Education was not venerated among the ruling class and, when it took place at all, it was in a foreign country. Work was also not a vocation of the nobility, who fought, hunted and nominally ran their estates. The higher ranks of the army, the government bureaucracy and the merchants were amply studded with foreign imports. Collectivism was established as the agricultural norm, especially in the North with its short growing seasons. Except for very brief periods, and despite a plethora of resources and low cost labor, Russia was a perpetual economic laggard.

THE BOLSHEVIKS:

The first revolution of February, 1917 was the one that toppled the Tsar. He abdicated on March 15. This revolution followed several months of intense worker unrest and resulted in the establishment of a Provisional Government appointed by the newly active Duma (legislature) whose composition had been restricted by the previous monarchy. The weak and ineffective Provisional Government ruled sometimes in concert with, sometimes at the sufferance of, the Petrograd Soviet (composed largely of industrial workers and the military) whose authority gradually spread throughout Russia. The Provisional Government undertook to continue the war, a generally unpopular stance, especially among the workers and military of the capital. This turned out to be an unexpected benefit for a relatively obscure, frighteningly focused former Social Revolutionary who had formed his own party. The Bolsheviks of Vladimir Ilych Ulyanov - Lenin - opposed the war and favored immediate peace as a step towards consolidating their power. This intrigued the Germans who sensed an opportunity to escape a two front conflict as well as acquire valuable territory. They financed the Bolsheviks, before and after their rise to power, and returned Lenin to Russia from his base in Switzerland. On October 24, 1917 the Bolsheviks and their allies took over control of the government, and of Russia.

Almost immediately the new Government moved to make peace with Germany (the Treaty of Brest-Litovsk was signed on March 3, 1918) and establish a single party, authoritarian state. Promised elections for a Constituent Assembly were diluted. A secret police mechanism was set up, copying Ludendorff's German system. After general demobilization a new military force, called the Red Army, was raised and organized by Leon Trotsky to combat opponents of Bolshevism. Even before the Civil War was settled in 1920, the army, in conjunction with the secret police, attacked and suppressed elements hostile to the urban worker-oriented Bolsheviks. These opponents were chiefly peasants who made up 80% of the population. Thus began a river of blood extending from Lenin and his police chief Dzerzhinskii to Stalin and his enforcer Beria that claimed millions of lives and saw millions more uprooted and transplanted. It separated peasants from urban workers, an occurrence that was to have far reaching consequences. It also marked one of the main differences between the Russian and Chinese revolutions. The peasant base of the Chinese Communist Party helped it to survive both politically and economically and gave it a broader foundation.

Economic understanding was not a feature of either Lenin's powerful mind, or that of any of his top subordinates. The intellectual Bolsheviks had spent extended periods in European cities but knew virtually nothing about the economy of Russia or even about economics as a science. Their first economic moves (e.g. nationalization of financial and industrial institutions, deliberate inflation, attempted abolition of money) were abysmal failures. As Paul Johnson wrote in Modern Times: "by the Spring of 1921, when the Kronstadt sailors rose[2], Lenin's whole economic policy, such as it was, lay in manifest ruins. Industry was producing practically nothing. There was no food in the towns. On Lenin's own admission tens and hundreds of thousands of disabled soldiers were becoming bandits. About the only thing in plentiful supply was the paper ruble, which the printing presses poured out ceaselessly, and which had now fallen to a little over one percent of its 1917 value - New Economic Planning was, in fact, surrender to the peasants and a return to the market system based on barter."[3] After the disastrous winter of 1921-22 Lenin's government, which had previously scorned assistance from the West, turned to the arch-capitalist Herbert Hoover and his American Relief Administration. In 1923 this organization responded with technical assistance and sixty million United States dollars, a gigantic sum for those days. Once again Russia had found itself dependent on Western assistance for its survival, a position that rapidly bred resentment and was reversed as soon as stability was achieved.

While United States aid temporarily staved off the crisis, it also had a more sinister long term result. It rescued the Bolshevik Government, as the Germans had done in 1918. An even more sinister event lurked nearby, a physically weakening Lenin suffered the first of a series of strokes in 1923, which allowed the Communist Party General Secretary Joseph Stalin to accumulate power. Following Lenin's death in 1924, Stalin first outmaneuvered, then liquidated all of his rivals, and assumed the role of leadership. Stalin accelerated the establishment of an even more centralized and repressive version of the Tsarist Empire. Purges took the lives of tens of millions. Social engineering on a massive scale rearranged the ethnic map. An abortive alliance with Germany in 1940 gave the Soviet Union a chance to gobble up parts of Romania, Poland and Finland. Domination of Eastern Europe followed heroic and costly efforts in World War II (the 900 day Siege of Leningrad alone cost one million lives) as did the spread of Leninist Bolshevism to portions of the Third World. At its height the Soviet empire (including its link with the People's Republic of China) included almost a third of the world's area and over one-quarter of its people.

Now this former empire is crumbling. Many of its newly independent entities are perilously close to collapse. An economic system, which many throughout the world had hailed as a pathway to the promised land, now lies in thoroughly discredited ruins. Central control has been shattered. Collectivism is being questioned. A thousand years of history has reached a hiccup. What does the future hold? Will Russia revive its economy and its empire? Will it implode into the hedgehog of defensiveness and suspicion that characterized the Muscovite, pre-Peter Tsardom?

TODAY:

The Soviet Union and its satellite states have disintegrated. We have seen the pictures of workers occupying the Lenin shipyard in Gdansk where Solidarity was born, of the Berlin Wall being dismantled, of businesses being auctioned to private buyers and new national flags being unfurled. But we have also seen violence surging between ethnic or political groups and the signs of economies spinning dangerously out of control. All are part of the new reality.

Things have changed dramatically in many visible ways. A visitor can travel virtually anywhere in the old Soviet Union without dealing with innumerable restrictions or the omnipresent Intourist guides. Photographs can be taken of almost anything. People will converse freely on a wide range of subjects without the hesitation born of fear. Military presence is noticeably less, and less officious where it exists. Evidence of the Communist Party - flags, insignia, statues, placards - has disappeared. Elections are taking place as is political debate. Some similarities to the Provincial Government era are striking.

Underneath the surface the changes are not nearly so pervasive. Conservatives, often older citizens, former Communist Party members and the military, consider the Soviet Union to have been needlessly humiliated and dismembered by liberal, Western-connected forces seductively advocating freedoms and riches that will only be available to an elite few. Russians do not normally react well to others' successes. Whereas in the West and most of Asia the prosperity of some acts as a motivator to the remainder, in Russia it usually arouses jealousy, suspicion and the desire to pull down, not emulate.

The intelligentsia, the ambitious former industrial managers, and black market operatives are among the few who view what has happened in the last few years as an unprecedented opportunity to think and do as they please - and to amass fortunes.

The vast majority of the people monitor an internal "Quality of Life" index and make their evaluations based upon its progress. For most people conditions have deteriorated badly. The Brezhnev years when everyone had a job, inflation was minimal, and the necessities of life were available increasingly, seem like the 'good old days' - even if the hidden core of society was progressively rotting away.

In the recent past Russian unemployment has skyrocketed, homelessness has become an urban problem, alcoholism has continued as an epidemic and prices have risen much faster than wages. Most people are struggling just to make ends meet under double digit monthly inflation. However, new market conditions have created some positive side effects. There are more products in the stores and lines have largely disappeared, although hoarding has continued and each harvest remains critical. Privatization has begun, and has proven successful for some smaller enterprises such as restaurants, shops and computer service bureaus. Entrepreneurial talents are appearing here and there. Substantial profits are being made by some. Religion is making a strong comeback after being suppressed under the Communist regime.

Other side effects are discouraging. Agriculture continues to be marginal. What food is produced is often retained on farms as a hedge against future famine and inflation, much as it was in the early 1920s. There are few with managerial skills and few trained industrial workers. Both inefficiency and slow conversion of factory capacity are hampering any build up of a private manufacturing sector. The government printing presses are running at full tilt, spewing out rubles and placing Russia on the brink of hyper-inflation, rendering moot such convertibility as legally exists.

Perhaps the most shocking development is the pervasiveness of criminality. Illegal activities, other than government corruption, used to be largely confined to the black market, and were imperfectly organized. Now they are everywhere, controlling much of the cash flow of Russia and its former Soviet Empire, especially in the areas of distribution and consumer products. These activities are highly organized. They are linked with growing Russian criminal organizations in places such as Israel and the United States. Collectively the underworld is called the 'Mafia'. The Russian 'Mafia' is forming connections with the international underworld to penetrate large scale criminal activities such as the drug business. The criminal influence has been boosted by the collapse of the ruble and the emergence of the United States dollar as the transaction currency of choice. The 'Mafia' have amassed billions of United States dollars, controlling or accessing much of Russia's supply. They have also been aided by the disgrace of the KGB, the stranding of military units in Eastern Europe and the military's destitute condition at home. These events have collectively provided trained recruits for illegal activities, which sometimes can be retained as units, nominally still in service. This powerful, extremely resourceful, criminal force will have influence over Russia's development, and will be especially difficult to bring under control.

The weakness of government is endemic from the national to the local level. Political organization is tenuous. Occasionally there is a popular figure, such as Boris Yeltsin, but this popularity rarely transcends the individual's person. Power-control of political, economic and military elements has flowed out of the center into the regions. Bureauocracy at all levels is staffed with former Communist Party apparat. Indeed this bears a similarity to the early years of Bolshevism when their bureaucracy was filled with former Tsarist officials. Like their predecessors of seventy years ago, the apparat's presence has fostered widespread distrust, extending that which they previously engendered as communists. If some type of free government is to succeed in Russia a new cadre of bureaucrats is needed. Also needed is an echelon of industrial managers. Most importantly, military officers and non-commissioned officers need to be both safely and productively integrated into the new society. This is a tall order, but retraining is one area that can respond to Western assistance.

What about economics? The critical food situation has been widely publicized and noted above. Just as critical is the scarcity of medical products, facilities, and trained personnel. Hospitals lack rudimentary equipment, such as disposable needles, and sometimes are without hot water. Doctors are often paid less than street cleaners. Any illness can have dire consequences.

Consumer goods, most of which are made in former defense plants, are of low quality and are generally high cost. There is no experience in their manufacture or distribution which is in any way analogous to that of the West, or for that matter, even to China.

There is no reliable economic statistical base. Figures were fudged for so long that economists have no idea what really happened. There have been recent efforts to improve the situation, but it will be a long time before statistical comparisons will have any validity.

The West, including the United States, has been arguing whether to send aid to Russia of $24 billion (much of it in the form of credits) over three years. Reliable analysts have projected that Russia needs a minimum of $100 billion per year for at least ten years to clean up its environment, stabilize the ruble, improve the infrastructure, begin to invest in plant and equipment, train managers, and stave off immediate economic disaster. Eastern Europe would require a like amount. Clearly this type of aid is neither forthcoming nor contemplated.

That brings into question the entire concept of the successful introduction and growth of free markets and democracy. The Gross Domestic Product (GDP) per capita of Russia and its sister states rank in the bottom tier of Europe, and is likely to stay there. While Baltic ports such as Gdansk, Riga and Talinn have a rich commercial history and have continued to maintain some economic contact with the outside world, Russia has no such history or contact. Centralization, paternalism, collectivized agriculture and rudimentary industry are its heritage. Any attempts to instill free market values and skills has to start from the ground up. It will be a gigantic task to keep Russia from falling further behind Europe. Catching up is not in the foreseeable future.

Many former Soviets and Eastern Europeans are voting in free elections for the first time in forty or fifty years. Russians are voting for the first time ever (discounting the tainted Constituent Assembly election of 1918). This is indeed progress. But what happens as the first blush of freedom fades and reality intrudes? This is taking place now. Will the desire for freedom be strong enough to overcome grave difficulties or will old patterns re-emerge?

At this moment the Russian economy is spiraling downward. The standard of living for most of its citizens is well below the levels of the last twenty years. Former Communist officials are filling most government positions. A new moneyed elite is being created by entrepreneurs, speculators and criminals. Russia's territory is smaller and its international prestige is lower than at any time since the Eighteenth Century. Will these conditions create the type of frustration and disillusionment which will be vented in the voting booth or in mass protests? Each citizen is asking himself or herself two questions: 1) Am I better off than before? and 2) What are the prospects for my descendants? The democratic process will have to deliver positive answers or a return to authoritarian government will be likely. The other struggle is between strong centralized government (whether it be through the executive or parliament) and religious rule. Can the center re-establish the power it held under the Tsars and the Bolsheviks? Will the regions grow increasingly autonomous? At the moment concrete answers seem a long way off.

What about foreign investment? It is true there are many potential opportunities. The Russian population is large - about 150 million. Resources abound. Labor costs are low. That is the good news. The bad news is that government is weak. Infrastructure is meager, especially in the area of transportation. There is no pool of skilled labor or management. The work ethic is low. Inflation is high and rising. The currency is worthless. Pollution is rampant. There is no history of private property. There is no established legal system. Acceptable returns on invested capital are at least a decade away.

TOMORROW:

In order to understand Russia's future two key forces must be explored:

1) Great Russian Nationalism
2) Islam

Together they will have more impact on the former Soviet Union that any other political, economic, or nationalistic trends.

Great Russian Nationalism has been a consistent factor in Russia since the rise of the Grand Duchy of Moscow in the Fifteenth Century. Great Russians (the Slavic, Scandinavian and Finnish blend that began in the Tenth Century) have passionately clung to the Orthodox faith, aggressively expanded, and arrogantly ruled at every opportunity. Physically they have generally moved east or south - rarely west. This latter tendency is likely to continue. Russia's food sources are mainly in the Black Earth Belt stretching from the Ukraine to the Urals. Oil is mostly to the south and southeast. Minerals lie east of the Urals. At no time since the Eighteenth Century has Russia been geographically as far from Europe as it is today. She is looking less and less in that direction.

Already there is a resumption of this southern and eastern orientation of Great Russian vital interests. Hostility and distrust of the West, always deeply seated in the Russian psyche, is likely to intensify with disappointment over financial aid. Military weakness created by pressure from the West, will increasingly rankle. The traditional fear of German hegemony in Central Europe, never far from the surface, will boil and prompt a search for buffers. Great Russian inherent insecurity, resentment over a lost empire, and frustration over spreading poverty will increasingly draw Russia away from European influence and towards Asia.

As Russia progressively turns eastward for its assistance and development, China, Japan[4], Korea, Taiwan, Hong Kong and other Asian economic powers will play a larger role in its affairs. They have a longer investment horizon than their Western counterparts and a greater need for Russia's resources. They also have less of a preconditional requirement for democratic government or free market characteristics. Therefore, as in the past, Great Russians will increasingly look Eastward to rebuild the core and strength of their homeland. As this strength begins to accumulate, the potential for conflict with those Asians exploiting or desiring Russian resources will escalate. Russia will progressively be drawn into Asian disputes as a potential ally with both natural resources and military power.

Russians will also seek to protect and reclaim their lost brethren. There are 150 million people in Russia. There are 25 million Russians in the Baltics, the Ukraine, Belorus, Kazakhstan, Moldova and Uzbekistan. Russian troops are currently stationed in all those areas. Russians remember that they once were the center of a vast empire, and now Russians who once ruled are subject to discrimination as well as humiliation in the empire's former outposts. This has already led to violence in the Baltics, Moldova, and Uzbekistan. There will be more, and it will last for many years.

There are numerous dissatisfied groups in Russia - including the Military and the KGB. While Russia has little history of military coups or military government, it has ample evidence of strongmen using military, or quasi-military, forces to control the populace and impose rule. If the economic situation doesn't improve; if criminal elements continue to control large swaths of the GDP; if the services that touch everyday lives continue to deteriorate - drastic action is likely. People crying out for something to be done are prone to turn to a strong central figure who promises results. A tradition of paternal, centralized, religious, and often dictatorial government exists. Thus will Russia most likely enter the Twenty-First Century, struggling for its existence and identity, with an increasingly authoritarian central government and a strengthening Orthodox church.

Another possibility exists - fragmentation. If central government continues to weaken regions will progressively consolidate local control. They may continue to set up independent states and make independent alliances, especially in the East. This could leave a poor, truncated European Russia west of the Urals. It would also create a less stable situation for world security than a larger, authoritarian state.

Eventually, Russia, united or fragmented, may have a role to play in a new world order, but for many years to come this role is likely to be peripheral. However, its borders will not be tranquil, this will be especially true where they touch the People's Republic of China and the Central Asian Islamic Republics.

Islam was an integral part of the former Soviet Union. Its presence in Central Asia can be traced to the Seventh Century, not too long after the establishment of the Muslim religion itself. This presence was built on a foundation of strong and independent states. Most people today barely recognize the names of the current Islamic nations: Kazakhstan; Kirgizia; Uzbekistan; Tajikistan; Turkmenistan; Azeribaijan, and Abkhazia - ranged across the old Empire's southern tier. Most of these Islamic peoples are ethnically Turkish. The vast majority are Sunni Muslim.[5] They are increasing rapidly. In the last years of the Soviet Union's existence one out of every two Soviet babies was born to Muslim parents. The Islamic population is growing at about 3.5% annually, and will roughly double by 2010, when over half of it will be under eighteen. There are now 60 million Muslims living in these new nations. By comparison, Turkey and Iran each have about 55 million inhabitants.

During their years in the Soviet Union Islamic people had their religion and their languages suppressed. In addition, their economic[6] and educational opportunities were minimized, their farm lands were exploited, their waters polluted, and their territory invaded by millions of ruling Russians. As a further blow, their young men were used as cannon fodder by the military to subdue Muslim brethren in Afghanistan.

Now that freedom has arrived there will be significant change. Already resources are being developed independently (for example, Kazakhstan has signed oil exploration deals with western companies to develop its reserves). Mosques are being rapidly constructed. Native languages have been reinstated. Importantly, for Islamic nations, institutions of higher learning, with religious foundations, are being established. Ties with Turkey and Iran are being formed. Hatred of the Russians, always smoldering, is beginning to flame, as is conflict between Muslims and non-Muslims. An additional risk factor is that Kazakhstan, and possibly Kirgizia are nuclear powers. All of the republics have their own military forces. Thus far their leaders have only briefly flickered onto the international stage, their conflicts are largely ignored and their origins are imperfectly understood. All of this will change.

Either Pan-Turkism or Islamic fundamentalism could catch fire and leap boundaries. Some or all of these republics could ultimately grow closer together, and maybe even become united? How unified, how fanatic, how hostile to Russia and to the West they will become are major questions for the future. Religious differences among these republics, and between them and the various segments of Islam, have been noted as an element of comfort to those discounting Islamic unity. These differences may well turn out to be less significant than many Western scholars currently project. In any event , this vibrant, resource laden, and strategically positioned sector is likely to become more important to the world as the Twenty-First Century approaches.

The future portends an authoritarian Russian state, initially introverted as it grapples with its own continuity. It will be less favorably disposed towards the West than it is now, and will have its economic growth and territorial integrity dependent on Asian conditions. As a price for economic support, Russia will be hard pressed to avoid being drawn into Asia's developing militarism.

To Russia's south and east will rise a turbulent, but increasingly influential, Islamic belt. Various alliances will form and reform along Asia's South Central Muslim kaleidoscope. This group of nations will most likely be hostile to Russia. But fending off Indian, Chinese or other incursions may, from time to time, bring a pause in hostilities. The region's importance, beyond resources, will lie in its location astride the Eastern gateway to Middle East oil and its contact with the boiling multitudes of China, India, Pakistan and Iran - not to mention Russia. Thus we can see two images emerging out of the ashes of the Soviet Union. One is of an introverted and truculent Russia, battling against both its own internal disequilibrium and the incursions from the attempted Chinese Asiatic hegemony. The other is the burgeoning significance of the Central Asian republics. As these dual entities elbow their way back into history's spotlight the consequences will reverberate. The former Soviet Union will be a major destabilizing factor in the world well into the next century.

---

1 William Wallace, *The Transformation of Western Europe* (Pinter, London ,1990).

2 they had become disenchanted with the revolution they helped to begin

3 Paul Johnson, *Modern Times* (Harper Perennial, NY, 1992) p. 93.

4 Settlement of the Kurile Island situations is presumed.

5 The 7 million Azeris and the 3.5 million Tajiks speak Farsi like the Iranians, are related to them ethnically and like them are Shiites.

6 The lowest GDPs per capita in the Soviet Union were in Uzbekistan and Tajikistan.

CHAPTER 2

The New Chinese Empire: A People's Republic Colossus?

At the other end of the erstwhile Second World is a country seemingly headed in the opposite direction from Russia - The People's Republic of China (PRC). To learn whether it can dominate the Orient in the Twenty-First Century as many predict, a glance at whence it came is required. Also required is an understanding of the Chinese feeling of superiority and universal centeredness. In addition, there has always been a Chinese suspicion of foreigners and a reluctance to allow them freedom of operation. Another characteristic has been the Chinese tendency to define their borders to include large swaths of their neighbors' territory. All of these elements are likely to be present in the years to come.

THE OLD EMPIRE

The history of China as a major, unified political entity begins sometime around 220 BC. At that time the Chin[1] Dynasty, under Emperor Shih Huang Ti and his chief minister Li Szu, consolidated most of what now comprises the modern nation. Roads, canals, fortifications, and the start of the Great Wall were created, binding and protecting the expanding territorial base. Conviction strengthened that the Chinese were a superior people inhabiting the Middle Kingdom, the cultural center of the universe. The bureaucratic system, which has since dominated Chinese government, sprouted on its way to omnipresence.

China has never been a land where religious fervor throbbed overtly as it has in Christian or Muslim nations. Its beliefs have been more cerebral, more interwoven with the every day life of family and politics and economics and behavior. These beliefs have also represented a philosophical mixture. The ingredients of this mixture and the ideological groundwork for China's religious future was laid with the lives of three contemporaries in the Fifth Century BC - Confucious, Lao Tsu (progenitor of Taoism), and Gautama Buddha. However, it wasn't until the Han Dynasty (which began in 206 BC) that these religious philosophies became established in China.[2] By the First Century A.D. all had entered the mainstream of the nation's activities where they have flourished ever since.

By several measures the height of Chinese civilization was attained during the Tang Dynasty (618 -907). This period has been aptly called the Chinese Renaissance. Its most brilliant light was Emperor Tai Tung who ruled from 627 to 649. During the Tang years Buddhism reached the apex of its influence. Poetry and sculpture achieved greatness. Painting and calligraphy were of extraordinary quality. Fiction, facilitated by the invention and spread of printing technology, was established as a literary form. The first book known to have been printed was published in 868. Despite their greatness, Tang accomplishments were known only regionally, the rest of the world remained largely unaware. A change was brewing. Europe and Central Asia were not long to remain ignorant of the great civilization being built to the East.

The most dramatic of the many incursions into China from the north occurred in 1205 when the Mongols, under their leader Temuchin, later called Genghis Khan (The Universal Emperor), made the first of their major attacks. North China was subdued in 1235 under Genghis' son Ogodai (Genghis had died in 1227) who established the Yuan Dynasty. Under Genghis's grandson, Kublai, all of China was incorporated under Yuan rule by 1279.[3] Meanwhile, the Mongols had established dominion from the Pacific Ocean to the middle of Europe by unleashing the world's most formidable fighting force, and overlaying it with a governmental system tinged with Chinese sophistication. The splendors of the Orient, formerly largely rumor, exploded into the West not only at the point of attack or from under the heel of the boot, but also from the tales of travelers. One such visitor was the Venetian, Marco Polo, who resided at Kublai's court from 1275 to 1292. Porcelain, poetry, gunpowder, noodles, silks, printing, and many other imported wonders opened European eyes to a civilization in many ways much more developed than their own. The Yuan Dynasty only remained in power until 1368, but the impact of Chinese culture upon the West was lasting.

In the estimation of most historians it was during the middle of the Ming Dynasty, around the year 1500, that Europe passed China as the world's most advanced civilization. At that point China contained about 125 million people, more than all of Europe combined, and it had a well developed bureaucratic system that had been in place for over one thousand years. But its dynamism was fading.

The rigidity of its social, political, and economic structures had begun to sap the nation's vitality and slow its relative growth. The development of modern China, however, didn't really begin until the crumbling of the Ming Dynasty in 1644. This occurred when another people swarmed out of the North to overwhelm China and had their leader assume the Mandate of Heaven. This time it was the Manchus, Jurchen people from Manchuria, who conquered, establishing the Qing Dynasty that was to last until the creation of a republic by Sun Yat Sen in 1912.

At first the conquest seemed similar to a process that had developed before. A new element came in, reinvigorated the country, flaunted symbols of its difference, and gradually was incorporated into the Chinese whole. This time, however, a new factor was introduced into the equation - Europeans.

Manchu rule rose to an early peak more or less traditionally, in the reign of Emperor Kangxi (1669-1722). Resistance was stamped out. Ethnic Chinese were required to shave their foreheads and grow queues as a mark of their subordination. Borders were expanded, including the first formal annexation of Tibet. A treaty with the Russians was executed. Strong central leadership was established.

Gradually, these accomplishments were eroded. War and plague reduced the population to about 100 million by 1700. Unrest spread. Central government weakened. In the reign of Emperor Qianlong, which was the longest in Chinese history (lasting from 1736 to 1799), the decline became manifest. Nevertheless, some significant accomplishments were recorded. The population, again on the rise, helped spread the introduction of foods of Western origin such as sweet potatoes, Irish potatoes, maize, and peanuts. Literature flowered, exemplified by the writing of China's most famous novel *The Dream of the Red Chamber.* But corruption, stagnation, and fragmentation prevailed, plunging Imperial China into its terminal illness. Many resistance movements, even indigenous independent communities flourished at this time, continuing a practice that was becoming traditional. One of the most interesting, the Taiping, originated in Guangxi around 1840. This community was egalitarian in nature, with authoritarian rule. It also was ascetic and founded upon Christian (Protestant) principles and extended important roles to women - including military combat.

There were elements of decay other than independence movements. Triads (secret societies often involved in criminal activity) were imported from Taiwan in the late Eighteenth Century and spread rapidly. Large numbers of Chinese began to move overseas in the 1850s to escape famine, depression, and war. Perhaps worst of all, opium was brought to the Mainland (mixed with tobacco) by soldiers returning from Taiwan around 1720. Europeans, especially the British merchants like Hong Kong based William Jardine, sensed a market opportunity and opium began pouring into China. By 1800 opium imports had reached 600,000 pounds. They grew sixfold by 1830 and then doubled again by 1839. At that point the Imperial government attempted to curtail addiction and ban opium products. This produced China's first large scale conflict with Europe, the Opium War of 1839 - 1842.

This war was a watershed. New technology burst upon medieval China. The British Navy arrived with steam driven ships and modern armaments, exposing the Imperial forces to humiliating defeat. Not only was the opium trade resumed, but the peace treaty granted the British, in addition to monetary compensation, the right for its nationals to reside in five coastal cities, and they were ceded Hong Kong island. The terms of this treaty were expanded in 1858, but prior to that had led to similar treaties with France and the United States. Wars between a resistant China and commerce-seeking powers also followed the Opium War. The French instituted a naval clash in 1884. The Japanese took Korea, Taiwan, and hunks of Northern China in 1894-5. The Boxer Rebellion of 1900 brought the joint military forces of several nations onto Chinese soil. Hegemony over Southeast Asia was lost to various European nations. Christian missionaries pored in to convert the 'heathen' Chinese. The Empire's frantic attempts to modernize and westernize both their military and industrial elements proved fruitless and destructive to their culture. By 1912 the last Qing Emperor had abdicated and Sun Yat Sen, as head of the Revolutionary Alliance, had become Provisional President of a Chinese Republic.

REPUBLIC, WAR, AND OCCUPATION

The pre World War II saga of the Chinese Republic was in most respects a continuation of the trends established in the final Imperial years. Central authority was weak and impecunious. Powerful local war lords usurped many governmental functions. Foreigners controlled large segments of the Chinese economy, and increased their territorial occupation. Attempts to bring industry and the military up to Western or Japanese standards were only marginally successful. Culture was partially severed from its historical roots by China's frantic efforts to propel itself into the modern world. The May Fourth Movement (May 4, 1919) was one such effort. Students and professors at Beijing University drew up a plan designed to reform China, subdue its Confucian principles, and make it a worthy participant in global affairs. Like many idealistic organizations this one was frustrated by the realities of governing, and its members drifted off into other areas. Many (such as Zhou Enlai) enrolled in the fledgling Chinese Communist Party.

Actual government in the 1920s and 1930s was notable more for the creation and ripening of the forces that were to influence post World War II China than it was for its running of the country.

Save for a brief flash of North-South unity under the Guomindang[4], following the military actions of 1928, the ebb and flow of warlord and foreign influence highlighted the story of the Republic. The Republic's prime progenitor, Sun Yat Sen, was an ephemeral leader. He led the Revolutionary Alliance. He transformed it into the Guomindang. He put the party in position to take power over the nation's 450 million people. But he was only an intermittent participant in governing prior to his death in 1925 at age 59. Two individuals did emerge from the morass of ideologies and party politics, which in China were messy and often deadly, and they were to tower over the nation for fifty years.

Mao Zedong was born to a Changsha farming family in 1893. He was largely self-educated, became exposed to Socialism as early as 1911, and was involved in the founding of the Chinese Communist Party in 1920. Although an important regional official, Mao bridled at increasing Soviet influence and at the alliance with the Guomindang encouraged by them. Expelled from his party posts and authority in 1927, he retreated to the mountains of Jiangxi. There he accomplished two things that would deeply affect the Party's future. First, he built peasant support, entirely different from the urban base that had sustained the Communist Party in China as it had in other areas. Second, he participated in the formation of the Red Army. By doing this Mao and his associates aroused the ire both of the Goumindang and the rest of the Chinese Communist Party. This antipathy turned to attempts at repression which culminated in the famous Long March; Mao's attempt to escape annihilation. The March started in Jiangxi in January, 1934 with 80,000 individuals. It ended in the Shanxi city of Yan'an in January, 1935 with 8,000 to 9,000 individuals. Yan'an would be the Party's main base until its successful bid for power following World War II.

The other individual, Chiang Kai-Shek was born to a merchant family in 1887. He received a military education in Japan and became an important commander in the Revolutionary Alliance forces. His network of connections, his marriage into the rich and influential Soong family, his direction of China's only officer training academy at Whampoa (outside Guanzhou) and his facility to manipulate lethal political forces led him to the top of the Goumindang by 1927. He remained there through its various incarnations for most of the time until his death in 1975.

The interplay between the Chinese Communist Party and the Goumindang in the 1930s fostered several key developments. It drove the communists to rely on peasant support as the Goumindang became established in the cities and it brought about the strengthening of the Red Army. It also encouraged Mao's faction to create a self-reliant, largely self-sufficient state in its Shanxi enclave. The Goumindang, in contrast, forged strong economic, military, and political links with foreigners; principally the Japanese and the Americans. These links, which developed into dependency, lasted throughout the party's existence.

The 1930s maneuverings of the Japanese set the stage for World War II's China Theater. The Japanese had moved into Korea and onto the Chinese mainland after the war of 1894-5. Their position was strengthened by victory in the Russo-Japanese War of 1904-5. Military activity spread following an armed clash in Manchuria in 1931. In 1932 and 1933 Japan established a formidable northern base there, which became the puppet state of Manchukuo in 1934. Fighting broke out between Japan and China on July 7, 1937. By 1941 all of the North, Northeast, and Central China was under Japanese control and had been formed into a series of puppet states. By the time the United States became involved in the war, Goumindang control had been compressed into an area of the Southwest, and the Chinese Communist Party was ensconced in its Northwest sanctuary. As the war against Japan progressed it became evident that Chiang's government, heavily backed by the United States, was as wary of their communist rivals as they were of the Japanese. The Chinese Communist Party, with little foreign backing (save a trickle from the Soviets), and only nominal connections with either the Goumindang or the Allied war effort, built a powerful fighting force on the nucleus of its Long March troops (the Eighth Route Army) which became battle tested against the Japanese.

Following the collapse of the Japanese, Chiang's forces became involved in a risky spreading of their strength. Their American advisors were anxious for the Goumindang to accept the surrender of the 1.25 million Japanese troops in China, as well as the 900,000 in Manchuria and control the 1.75 million Japanese civilians residing throughout the country. This advice encouraged Chiang to follow a strategy of widely dispersing his forces in an attempt to rapidly consolidate the entire country under his rule. This effort started with a thrust into Manchuria in 1945.

Chiang's strategy ran afoul of Mao and his followers, who refused to cede control of their military (that was now collectively called the People's Liberation Army), or their peasant political base. To make the situation worse for the Goumindang government, hyper-inflation broke out in the war ravaged economy. The result was that Chinag's over-extended forces were routed in civil war. By October 1, 1949 the People's Republic of China was born, Mao ruled Beijing and Chiang's base had been reduced to Taiwan.

THE NEW EMPIRE

The Mandate of Heaven descended upon the new emperor, Mao Zedong, and his People's Republic. Like their Bolshevik counterparts, the Chinese Communist Party spent the first few years, after triumphing in civil war, consolidating and extending their power. Over 1 million "landlords" were exterminated in the course of land redistribution. The party's goal was to establish control over every facet of the nation's existence. It had largely accomplished this by the mid-1950s.

Relations with the two post-War superpowers were volatile and convoluted. The United States had an ingrained distrust of communism and from the beginning kept its distance. Even during the war with Japan, United States support for Mao was no more than nominal. After the Japanese surrender, and particularly after the establishment of the People's Republic, virulent anti-communist forces took over American foreign policy. They backed Chiang, protected Taiwan, withheld recognition of the People's Republic, and disciplined officials who had sympathized with Mao or predicted his triumph. The United States viewed the People's Republic as part of a communist monolith threatening the existence of democracy. This view was highlighted in the famous April, 1954 confrontation between John Foster Dulles and Zhou Enlai at the

Geneva talks, which were attempting to end the French-Vietnamese conflict. Thus, for a brief period in the 1950s the United States' attitude actually encouraged maintenance of the very monolithic alliance it sought to prevent.

The People's Republic's relations with the Soviet Union were problematic. Soviet agents had been involved in the Chinese Communist Party's creation and through them Moscow attempted to control party policy and actions, and reinforce its urban orientation. Mao and his compatriots opposed this and they continued to fight Soviet influence. At several critical points American intransigence forced Communist China into a position of closeness with the USSR which was beyond its preferred comfort level. One point was during World War II, when the vast majority of Allied support went to Chiang and the Goumindang. Another was in the immediate post-War period, when the need to organize the Chinese state and set up an economic model arose. A third was during and after the Korean War (begun without Chinese knowledge) when it became evident that the People's Liberation Army had to be re-organized and modernized to perform at anything approaching world standards. At all of these times the United States treated the People's Republic as if it were an enemy firmly in the Soviet camp, and by doing so helped to place it there and establish Soviet economic, political, and military models.

All of these points came into focus in the period of 1953-57 which was an epic formative period. It contained the First Five Year Plan, which was largely successful, and the reorganization of the military. Both followed Soviet models. This period was virtually the only time when the dreaded communist monolith actually existed. At other times there was a more varied picture. Mao made his first visit outside China to Moscow in December of 1949 (the occasion was Stalin's 70th birthday celebration). He spent several days ignored by all Soviet officials, a severe loss of face. Nevertheless, the Chinese Communist Party accepted vital Soviet assistance and adopted Stalinism as its model. As seen in China, Nikita Khrushchev's unannounced (to Mao) attacks on Stalin in early 1956 started unraveling the alliance as it attacked the foundations of communist orthodoxy. The history of armed conflict between the countries was renewed in fighting on the Amur River border in 1969. Since then the People's Republic and the Soviets enjoyed only brief instances of cordiality. After Yugoslavia's 1948 break from Moscow's influence, the growing antagonism of the 1950's marked the initial signs of the unraveling of the Second World. For a long time this was only dimly perceived in the West. During the following decades two separate centers of communist power developed. Even they vanished with the splintering of the Soviet Union leaving the People's Republic the sole major bearer of the communist torch.

As a government leader Mao believed in periodic chaos. He liked to shake up the status quo, ostensibly to regenerate the spirit of revolution. Another objective, undoubtedly, was to strengthen his power base. Most such moves were spectacular and costly failures. The two outstanding examples were the Great Leap Forward and the Cultural Revolution. The Great Leap thinking grew out of drafting the Second Five Year Plan which was to last from 1958 to 1962. Mao proposed radical measures, such as pervasive agricultural collectivization, and creation of a massive People's Militia. The first caused widespread famine. The second proved totally impractical. In the wake of these expensive failures Mao stepped down as Head of State (although not as Chinese Communist Party Chairman) in 1959.

The Cultural Revolution began in the spring of 1966. 'Old elements' of the party and society were purged. Red Guards created from the ranks of students and other youth seized control of many organizations. Economics, education, and most everyday activities ground to a halt. Massive displacements of population took place. After a brief taste of power the Red Guards began to get out of control. Cultural Revolution policies became recognized as pervasively disastrous. The People's Liberation Army was called upon to restore order starting in February of 1967, a feat it finally accomplished by August 1968. Mao's power declined with the collapse of the Cultural Revolution and continued at a reduced level until his death on September 9, 1976 (eight months after the death of Zhou Enlai).

From 1954 until the Cultural Revolution internalized its energy, the People's Republic attempted to become a major force in the Third World. It organized conferences, supported local communists, and dispensed both economic and military aid. Once the Cultural Revolution turmoil receded it partially renewed these efforts. The results were essentially threadbare, with People's Republic backed governments falling and centrally planned economies failing. Outside of annexing Tibet, military expansions were equally fruitless. The Korean War, the clashes with the Soviets, the 1962 Invasion of India and the invasion of Vietnam in 1974, all exposed Chinese military weaknesses and provided no enduring results. The People's Republic began to rethink its principles and directions.

After Mao's death new leaders with new perspectives assumed power. Hua Gofeng presided over the initial thawing towards the West. Deng Xiaoping continued it, and in 1979 stressed the family farm as the main agricultural unit, freeing farm prices to the vagaries of the market. He subsequently created fourteen open (to trade and development) coastal cities and five special economic zones. This prompted widespread reform. The People's Republic of China joined the United Nations in 1971 and received its noted visit from President Richard Nixon early in 1972. Real growth in the economy accelerated with the allowance of more private enterprise. It averaged almost 9% annually from 1978 through 1992, the highest rate of growth in the world. The population crossed the 1 billion mark in 1982 (463 million were 18 and under) and state controlled industrial production dropped from 78% in 1978 to 50% by 1992.

All of this didn't take place without conflict, abuses, and regressions. The most outstanding was the confrontation in the Spring of 1989 between the students gathered in Beijing's Tienamen Square[5], and elements of the People's Liberation Army called in by party hardliners. The economic liberation that started with private farms and special economic zones has continued to build. Social, educational, and political freedom has grown more sporadically, and in some areas not at all. But by 1992 China's economic history and early experiments with private enterprise had given its 1.2 billion people a diversified economic output valued at between one-quarter and three-eighths of the United States.[6] It is a nuclear power (since October 1964) with the world's largest military force (over 3 million), significant hard currency reserves, and a burning desire to impact world events.

THE FUTURE: CONFUSION OR COLOSSUS?

The *Economist* in its survey of China of November 28, 1992, posed the question, "What will happen when a fifth of mankind, already the biggest producers of large numbers of industrial and food products, really start industrializing and exporting?" The numbers are formidable. Some experts estimate that China's Gross Domestic Product by the year 2000 could be eight times that of 1978 and on the way to equaling that of the United States by the middle of the Twenty-First Century. Cities like Beijing, Guanzhou, and Shanghai, as well as the special economic zones, already throb with economic activity and bulge with foreign investment. There are 15 million private companies now in China with more being formed every day. Consumer products are made in volume, for domestic use as well as export, and stores are stocked with imported goods.

Despite many setbacks, the People's Republic seems to have survived the stress of conflict and seems favorably placed to thrive in the coming century. What can derail it? The creation of new ruling cadres to replace those currently in power will present challenges. Overcoming critical shortages of services (especially in the banking and legal areas), building transportation and communication infrastructures, and dealing with the inevitable high inflation will stretch the nation's capabilities. The economic growth rate will surely slow. The Chinese Communist Party may have to be ideologically transformed, or even replaced. The power of the People's Liberation Army (political, economic, and military) is increasing in reward for its 1989 support. Even with all these cross currents, the only two conditions likely to prevent China from attaining the above projections are internal disruptions and war.

Chinese government has always been authoritarian and heavily bureaucratized. It is likely to remain so. China has only occasionally spouted ideological intensity, but often radiated economic and military expansionism. Neighbors in all directions could feel this intensity, especially if they are included within the borders of 'greater China'. Distrust of foreigners and foreign control, always inherent in the Chinese, will remain strong. If a need develops for foreign investment and assistance this could deepen into resentment. Self-sufficiency will become a byword, as it has many times in the past. Thus it seems probable that China will not long tolerate foreign influence, will seek to cow its neighbors, and may well display spurts of aggressive expansionism, both as to influence and to actual territory. There is an arms race brewing. Asia is full of military powers arming at a furious rate. China is in the middle of them, and is upgrading its own armed forces. Asia will not be a peaceful place in the upcoming century.

Several points of internal dissension are likely to arise. The battle between central control and local autonomy has long been waged in China. It is going on today. This is especially true in the prosperous Southeast, bubbling with the spirit of independence, which awaits the inclusion of Hong Kong in 1997. Both the influence of the Chinese Communist Party and the country's ultimate unity depend on the outcome of the tug-of-war between Beijing and Guanzhou. There will be other abrasions. Disputes could arise from multiracialism and multiethnicity, particularly on China's Western marches. Ethnic subjugation, population transplants, and cultural erasure have occurred there for centuries. Continuation of all of these forces will give rise to persistent causes for unrest, turmoil, and intervention.

Collision with the flinty religious edges or the demographic pressure cookers positioned on its borders will create external challenges for the People's Republic, or its successors.

China will be severely tested. It has entered the 1990s with more promise and unity than at any time since the reign of Kangxi. But the new century will be very difficult. The most likely result is that China will not emerge united enough, from internal struggles and prolonged warfare, to have a real chance at becoming a colossus until well into the century's latter half.

While there is no more Second World in the post-World War II sense, there will be new international permutations and combinations involving former Second World countries, or portions thereof. These interactions will significantly impact the events unfolding in the coming century.

---

1 Spelling of Chinese Words (for Western consumption) is both in the old and new manner. This is not designed to confuse, but to reflect the usage prevalent prior to Western incursions (old style) and post Manchu (new style) when Europeans were relatively numerous.

2 Buddhism was the only foreign religious intellectual import of significance for centuries.

3 The first time it had been united under non-Han-Chinese control.

4 National People's Party founded by Sun Yat Sen and ultimately controlled by Chiang Kai-Shek.

5 Initially to honor former party Secretary General Hua Yaobong who had been deposed in 1987 for being too reform oriented.

6 Valuation depends on currency conversion and other economic statistics which are inexact.

The First World Flounders

Outwardly, at the apex of its supremacy, the First World is subcutaneously besieged. Its reigning superpower, the United States, is a case in point. While attempting to settle disputes in many overseas locales and proselytize political and economic theory, it finds itself financially strapped at home, struggling to find answers to surging demographic imbalances, and trying to upgrade both its decaying essential services and its infrastructure. The future of the First World will be epitomized by that of the United States. If the United States becomes an isolated sphere of influence, marooned in a sea of turmoil and rising Third World power, this predicament will likely be mirrored, or exceeded by the experiences of spheres centered in Germany and Japan. Again, history can be prescient. Civilizations throughout time have grounded on shoals remarkably like those of today. Inspection of First World conditions and attitudes can assist in projecting its equilibrium into the coming century.

CHAPTER 3

Technology: Monster or Messiah?

We live in an era of sophisticated technology that has penetrated into every interstice of the Industrialized World. Integrated circuits are ubiquitous. Virtually all households have a telephone and a television. Motor vehicles clog the streets and have fostered networks of highways. Sophisticated instrumentation has become ensconced in nearly every vocation and avocation, particularly via the computer.

This technological age is arrogant. Its progeny confidently believe they can settle in any location, confront any obstacle, combat any disease and, largely due to the wonders of technology, emerge victorious. John F. Kennedy summed it up when he said, "Problems created by man can be solved by man." In many ways they can, and technology has delivered wonders, often beyond even the wildest dream.

This is not an unmixed blessing, We have forgotten, or chosen to disremember, "that the world once lived and grew without adding machines and newsprint and brick-walled streets and the tyranny of clocks"[1] We congratulate ourselves that today's life in the West is longer and more fulfilling than ever before. We are convinced that we are riding the crest of a technological wave, which, as it reaches less fortunate sands, will improve lives there as well.

That is the credo of the First World. It has probed space. It has brought irrigation and bountiful production to former deserts, like Southern California. Through the miracle of air conditioning it has created a giant metropolis in Houston, where formerly heat and humidity discouraged habitation. It has held back the raging waves of the North Sea from Holland and Zealand with complex dikes and hydraulic pumps. It envisions technology combating and defusing powerful phenomena, such as major earthquakes, or meteors headed towards this planet, or deadly cancer cells. But this credo has also brought acid rain, health threatening magnetic fields, choking smog, invasive information gathering, and a plethora of other ills that plague us daily. As a society we have narrowed our focus and in most instances, "can conceive of a remedy only within the limits of technology."[2]

Have we undermined the moral, ethical, and philosophical bases of our civilization? Czeslaw Milosz writing in the early 1950s felt keenly that we had. "The masses in highly industrialized countries like England, the United States, or France are largely de-Christianized. Technology, and the way of life it produces, undermines Christianity far more effectively that do violent measures."[3] If one substituted the word 'faith' for Christianity it becomes evident what a mess we are in - adrift with no anchor, no navigation, indeed no hope other than more technology. Technology has thus become both a messiah and a monster.

What can be done? How can we overcome urban decay, environmental pollution, inadequate health care, and other massive challenges to our way of life? Václav Havel's answer is clear. "Our attention, therefore inevitably turns to the most essential matter: the crisis of contemporary society as a whole, the crisis that Heidegger describes as the ineptitude of humanity face to face with the planetary power of technology. Technology is out of humanity's control, has ceased to serve us, has enslaved us and compelled us to participate in the preparation of our own destruction. And humanity can find no way out; we have no idea and no faith, and even less do we have a political conception to help us bring things back under human control."[4] He implies nothing less than the recapture and re-establishment of the soul in our society as our only hope for redemption.

There is more than one type of efficiency. There is the type that makes products, services, or industries cost less or operate better. There is also the type that makes society as a whole function more smoothly or be more friendly to its inhabitants. Those countries, at the heart of the Technological Age, have consistently strived for the former at the expense of the latter. It is time for some temporization, some trend reversal.

Mechanization has progressively removed skilled jobs from industrial nations, opened up opportunities largely in the lower paying service industries, and created higher endemic levels of unemployment. Most product 'improvements' have left in their wake unanticipated side effects ranging from toxic waste to invasion of privacy. Despite the initial positive readings, development does not ultimately create efficiency for those societies which have to deal with threats such as oil tankers cruising close to their coasts and chemicals lurking in their food supplies. Technology doesn't always have to be counter-productive. For its age to flourish the wonders of the laboratories need to be more comprehensively beneficial. They need to nestle within the confines of inherent beliefs, to be powered by a deep societal soul, not just integrated circuits. We need to do more evaluation before rushing to implement the latest technical advance. A more thoughtful society can be a more comprehensively productive one. That end is not yet out of reach, but it is growing more difficult.

Two theories of modern physics illustrate the complexity of this task: 1) quantum mechanics, and, 2) chaos theory. "In general quantum mechanics does not predict a single definite result for an observation. Instead it predicts a number of different outcomes and tells us how likely each of these is. . . Quantum mechanics therefore introduces an unavoidable element of unpredictability or randomness into science."[5] As if that concept isn't enough to destabilize our view of the technological world, one more element is there to confuse us and make analysis more difficult. "Chaos theory understands that a small change may be magnified in a series of cascading events. . . the premise of chaos theory is that you can't predict in a straight line; you have to simulate with complex equations that account for feed back."[6] We now find ourselves in a technological hall of mirrors, where nothing is as it appears, and all the pathways are concealed. No wonder ordinary citizens feel that they can no longer adequately analyze issues. No wonder we rely on so-called 'experts' and sound byte summaries of information. No wonder that so many industrial/technological inhabitants seem rootless and insecure.

As Havel implies, the way out involves going back to bedrock as individual beings. In order to extricate ourselves from the overly technological mire and temper 'advances' that turn out counterproductive, we need to rearrange both priorities and lifestyles. We need to better learn how to use the marvels of technology rather than having them employ us. We need to develop belief in something other than the power of human-driven technology. While this is possible, it must be candidly acknowledged that it is unlikely within the confines of our present industrialized society. Our inner core can be reconstituted only if we can forego the initial impulse to search for yet another technology to counteract the impact of existing ones. If we can build internal strength in place of reliance on external assistance, then this civilization has a chance to extend its life, and its span. If not, the whirlpool will consume it, and a new civilization, based on principles not unlike those that founded our own, will ultimately take its place.

In order for us to properly evaluate this civilization's vitality, it will be necessary to inspect some of the First World's inner workings. Currently brooding amid the wonders of technology, like the winged figure of humanity in Durer's famous engraving, *Melancholia I*, this world is struggling to rouse and energize itself so that it can cope with the ambiance it has created.

It shouldn't be implied that technological advancement is evil per se. Medicine, communications, transportation, and many other aspects of each world citizen's daily life has been enriched by the massive developments of the last few decades. Many problems deemed hopeless or insurmountable have been conquered by the efforts of science. Many more will be as well. It is a question of degree and direction and, above all, deity. Will we continue to worship at the altar of technology or will we make it a tenet of a larger faith? Can we cease regarding technology as a messiah in order to prevent it from becoming a monster? The answer will determine the First World's destiny.

---

1 Beryl Markham , *West With the Night* (Bantum Books, 1978) p. 38.

2 Václav Havel, "Politics and Conscience," *Open Letters,* ed. Paul Wilson (Vintage Books, 1991) p. 252.

3 Czeslaw Milosz, *The Captive Mind* (Vintage International Edition, 1990) p. 212.

4 Václav Havel, "The Power of the Powerless," *Open Letters* (Vintage Books, 1991) p. 206.

5 Stephan W. Hawking, *A Brief History of Time* (Bantum Books, 1988) pp 55-6.

6 Esther Dyson, "Physics for Economists," *Forbes*, October 16, 1989, p. 266.

CHAPTER 4

A Bankruptcy of Precepts

The rot infesting the pilings upholding Western civilization has accelerated its rate of growth during the post World War II period. The infestation has spread throughout much of the world, tainting its prospects for successful industrialization and democratization. The reason is that the basic precepts needed to support any civilization have begun to decay in the First World.

The disease's most virulent outbreak is in the vast urban areas that have become an epidemic inside many nations. Experts project that by the turn of the century, "for the first time in history more people will live in and around cities than in rural areas."[1] While cities have presented problems to societies for millennia, at no time have their maladies presented a greater collective challenge. This is due to their increased relative size. The inability of Western civilization to come to grips with the economic, social, environmental, and political complexities of urban living is the single largest threat to its viability.

One hundred years ago intellectuals in the United States fought a battle over urban ills, and were at least partially successful. Incipient muckrakers who wandered the world "came home believing along with James Bryce, author of *The American Commonwealth,* that the government of cities is the one conspicuous failure of the United States."[2] That belief is even more true today, and is applicable over most of the globe. At the same time that people have flocked to larger and larger urban areas, the mechanisms for dealing with their safety, their health and their well being have corroded. There is no question that the contest to preserve and expand the Western-based way of life will be waged in innumerable metropoli. The city dwelling Maya lost such a struggle a thousand years ago and their civilization temporarily vanished. The challenge is equally formidable and equally critical for urbanites of the late Twentieth Century.

Crime rages almost unchecked in many cities. Rio de Janeiro is only one of many examples. Soot and smog often makes the air unbreathable in Denver, Mexico City, and Eastern Europe. Rubbish piles proliferate, reclaiming large sections of places such as Lima and Calcutta. Crumbling buildings plague Cairo and abandoned ruins dot areas of New York giving them the appearance that large scale warfare has just ended. Drugs, homelessness, and pollution of air and water are endemic, crimping existence and spreading fear. Complete systemic breakdowns have hit Kinshasa and Beirut, among others. However, the picture is not all bleak. There are success stories, such as Curitiba, Brazil, where decay has been arrested, even reversed. Nevertheless, the combined powers of capitalism, democracy and technology have not yet solved the puzzle of urban living. The world's cities, and now the bulk of its population, are at least as vulnerable to disease, natural disaster, dissipation, and dissatisfaction as ever. Thus, the very magnitude of its collective urban areas will prove the industrial/technological civilization's major obstacle, and possibly its downfall.

Hand in glove with the growth of technology and the cities is the concept of progress, which arrived in the Eighteenth Century and now looms over the entire First World. It has become a fundamental tenet of Western life that prosperity and success depends upon increasing profits, amassing ownership of goods and services, and expanding personal freedom. Attainment of these ends has become the definition of progress for our society. Technology, individuality, and consumption have all become idols to be worshipped. For a long time these idols gratified their admirers. This trend may have run its course in most industrial nations which are satiated with goods and privilege.

The image of material progress has become overlaid, and often obfuscated, by periodic attempts at income redistribution, by the provision of comprehensive social services, and by battles with technological side effects. These are signs that the concept is being redefined. Mere maintenance of current living standards is becoming a more widespread, if defensive objective. In a growing number of instances traditional 'progress' may also have bumped up against physical limitations. The size and proliferation of cities has created one limitation. Another is the delicate balance between demography and industrialization. Christopher Lasch, who compiled a definitive study of progress, pointed out that, "in view of the present rate of population growth, the attempt to export a Western standard of living to the rest of the world, even if it was economically feasible in the first place, would amount to a recipe for environmental disaster."[3] The search for ecological and sociological equilibrium has sparked a debate. One side clamors for population control in the Third World in order to ensure environmental preservation. The other seeks to put the onus on the plethora of First World industrial products and processes. There are no absolute answers, only tortuous and delicate compromises. Convoluted debates and trade-offs are not characteristics of a civilization in the full flower of expansion, but rather are symptoms of the ever-narrowing options in a struggle for survival. Nevertheless, the very process of questioning is healthy, and properly handled may prolong Western civilization's existence.

Progress has had another comprehensive and restricting consequence. Financial flexibility has disappeared into the maw of the insatiable consumer. There are few creditors left. The industrial nations, like the Third World, are awash in debt, prisoners of appetites beyond their means. The financial powers of the post war years: the United States; Germany; Japan; Saudi Arabia, have all progressively fun afoul of ambitions that exceeded their resources, and drained their coffers. Taxes are rising, spending is being microscoped, priorities are being rearranged - everywhere. Will the measures that are currently politically acceptable prove to be enough? Can the financial integrity that spawned the Industrial and Technological Revolutions be restored? This is an additional rampart for our civilization to surmount and one which trumpets the need for life style alterations.

Two offspring of progress - the media and litigation - have complicated matters, particularly in the United States. In 1733 John Peter Zenger was brought to trial, but won the right to print in his New York Weekly Journal material that was critical of the New York Gazette. He won this right because the information to be printed was true. This trial has correctly been sited as the precedent for a free press in what became the United States of America, eventually the media center of Western civilization. A little-remembered fact is that the *Gazette* was an organ of the colonial government. Until quite recently media was regularly utilized to promote the opinions of particular interest groups. While it may have been free, the press made no pretense of being objective. Lately, media has become regarded as a cradle of objectivity, a discoverer of wrongdoing, an arbiter of issues, and a national conscience. Citizens look to the media, and increasingly to television, not only to entertain but also to simultaneously unravel the complexities of modern living, instantly report global events, and provide brief summaries of each societal nuance. This is a tall order, maybe too tall. It has led to a reliance upon imagery. It has increased pressure to render instant opinions. It has shortened attention spans. Despite the information explosion and extension of media reach, citizens are less thoughtfully informed, less able to analyze complex problems, and more subject to the suggestion of imagery than ever before.

All of these conditions have continually been present to a degree in intensely political, often impatient countries, like the United States. But the media-dependence has deepened. For example, Cable News Network reaches into every cranny of the globe. Its cameras were even awaiting the first American troops landing on the beaches of Somalia in 1992. Ironically, this pervasiveness of media has led the First World away from its freedom and its principles. Privacy is proving hard to protect. The public has become attuned to instant gratification, become easier to manipulate, become less well read, even less literate and become more accustomed to information as entertainment. This is not what Zenger desired. Media has become a purveyor of excess technology and intellectual sloth. The public's engorgement on a seemingly endless feast of data has produced a general procedural ossification and not provided the tools for more rapid responses to challenges.

Currently there are 780,000 lawyers in the United States (one for every 320 citizens) up from 260,000 in 1960. There are 209 million suits filed in state courts alone each year. The direct costs (settlements, awards, fees) of the tort system is $185 billion per year, up from $46 billion as recently as 1980.[4] Corporations in the United States spend $21 billion annually on product liability insurance premiums alone. This is approximately ten percent of their total pre-tax profits. All of these are results of an eruption of litigation in the world's most litigious society, This affects every aspect of American life, including health care costs, transportation costs, and property taxes. Through osmosis it has impacted the rest of the world. The costs of doing business, of governing, of existing have all been boosted by litigation, an American export.

It is correct that Western Civilization was built upon the rule of law. No one recognized this more than Judge Tapping Reeve, educator of many of this country's eminent early jurists. He noted in 1813 that, "theoretically courts make no law, but in point of fact they are legislators." This has not always been a bad thing. Many of the West's most illustrious figures were lawyers and many of its most admirable principles can be directly attributed to the law. But, increasingly, so can its legislative and administrative constipation. Statutes are made by and for lawyers. Policy is expected to be settled by litigation. Civil court calendars are clogged by frivolous suits. The costs of damages raise the price of goods and services. The fact that Americans have developed, "a tendency to frame nearly every social controversy in terms of a clash of rights impedes compromise, mutual understanding and the discovery of common ground."[5] So does the apparent necessity to attach blame in every facet of daily life, at every level of society.

Nowhere is this more evident than in the area of property. As our civilization has grown more prosperous, and more materialistic, it has increasingly resorted to the law for the acquisition and protection of assets. In the ever-expanding assertion of individual rights, a growing number of them seem to revolve around the concept of ownership. This has led us to a perilous point, identified by Alexis de Toqueville one hundred and fifty years ago. "When the right to property was merely the basis for other rights, it could easily be defended, or rather it was not attacked: it was like the encircling wall of society whose other rights were the advance defense posts. . . When it no longer has the cover of other more doubtful and more hated rights, it is in great danger. Soon the political struggle will be between the Haves and the Have Nots; property will be the battlefield."[6]

The most severe psychological blow is that many of our cherished precepts have lost substance as our civilization matured. First of all, is the tragic fact that the family unit has come apart in the First World. Paul Johnson argues persuasively[7] that this process started in the early Eighteenth Century. Whenever it started, the process has accelerated in the post-World War II period. With it has gone some of our system's strongest underpinnings. A republican icon, Jean Jaques Rousseau, declared in 1762, "the most ancient of all societies, and the only one that is natural, is the family." From its inception the United States has counted among its most solid pillars of support the extended family, the family farm, and the family business. All are growing weaker. In America the divorce rate now equals the marriage rate. Twenty-four percent of all heads of households under thirty are single mothers. The figure is fifty-eight percent in African-American households Out of the 4 million births in the United States each year, one million are to single mothers. Over 340,000 children annually are being raised outside the homes of either of their natural parents. One out of every five Americans lives alone.

The elderly are often ensconced in isolated communities, placed there by relatives, or dependent upon the nation's largess. They exist without the emotional or the financial support of a family. The vital interaction between old and young that has nurtured and sustained so many societies has largely been eclipsed in the Industrial World. A cult of youth has assumed control of corporations, government bureaus and educational institutions. The wisdom of elders that used to counsel is not only ignored, it is increasingly reviled.

This condition is exacerbated as the sequestered demographic extremes - the very old and the very young - advocate policies that are mutually antithetical. Resources and policies are increasingly strained by the needs of these groups. In countries, like the United States, with an aging work force, laborers will be asked to support growing numbers of retirees. At the same time the elderly, perceiving a threat to their cherished benefits (many of which serve as family replacements), oppose funding the education of those who will be called upon to support them. Youthful voters, despairing of ever collecting benefits in old age, view these as siphoning the lifeblood from their prospects and call for their reductions. In this manner First World economic and social forces have combined to stress the civilizational tectonic plates, widening the fault lines, increasing the risks.

Along with the uncoupling of the family links has come an unprecedented quest for individual freedom. Such freedom is in many ways admirable, and is advocated in our civilization's seminal documents. But, as with the spread of cities, the growth of technology and the proliferation of information, individuality has been overdone, relative to the health of the community. Christopher Lasch has encapsulated the problem, "Starting as if from one terminus of history, from a condition of society in which all the relations of persons are summed up in the relations of family, we seem to have steadily moved towards a phase of social order in which all these relations arise from the free agreement of individuals."[8]

One example of this situation is the 'liberation' of women. Women now account for forty percent of the Western work force. In Europe over forty-four percent of recent college graduates are women. In the United States fifty-eight percent of all families have two wage earners. Sixty-five percent of all women with children are in the work force. These figures all represent geometric progressions over the past thirty years. By themselves they all can be counted as positive achievements. Combined with many other elements of attempted individuality they can add up to societal rootlessness, even disintegration. In the process of removing barriers for both men and women societal foundations have been damaged as well. After all the angst and effort we can still ask the question. Have women really been 'liberated' from the sins of the past and given opportunity for the future? Have the textures of our families and our societies really been improved? We have undone many injustices and opened doors in the process, but we haven't yet begun the arduous task of effectively redefining and reconstituting families in the context of their attendant communities. As these tasks are underway the fast forward button of our technological lives has not been released to allow for reflection and healing. Women at all socio-economic levels, along with their new jobs and freedoms are experiencing physical and psychological disorientation.

This is only one instance of many where, in the process of pursuing genuinely felt good intentions, we may have wandered away from the nexus of social interaction. What has happened is that, merited or not, when dashed against civilizational pillars the collective impact of "too much freedom, suddenly, is like too much wine on an unaccustomed stomach. It deranges; it confuses; it enflames; it finally destroys."[9] As a society we have moved ruthlessly towards our objective of greater individuality and greater freedom. This has produced its share of destruction, and families are directly in its path.

What has suffered most is the sense of community. In tribal cultures, "basically, each self did not exist alone or separately, but rather as a facet of the larger, interconnected whole embodied by the society."[10] This was, and is, one of the strongest elements of tribalism. It was also one of the basic strengths of Western civilization in both its formative and its growth years. To the extent that communities have been lost our civilization has been weakened. Loss of a sense of community on top of the weakening of family has inflicted more damage than merely splitting society into a multiplicity of fractions. One of its most insidious manifestations has been the metastasizing tumors of privation embedded in the midst of rampant prosperity.

Poverty has been around forever, but it is especially dangerous for it to spread in a society where material success is valued so highly and where it is being achieved by some so visibly. The ideal culture for privation's rapid growth is the miasma of the inner city. Whether it be newly unemployed Eastern Germans or urban African-Americans, "it's dangerous to have a bunch of people in a society who've got nothing to lose."[11] All nations are feeling the effects. With more citizens than ever who feel they have nothing to lose, and without those communal values that once sustained and protected them, many nations are beginning to reel under the weight of bearing poverty and its accouterments.

Is there a remedy? There is. It will involve redressing the balance that has swung too precipitously towards individual rights and freedoms and away from communal well being. But it will take even more than that. Three other key precepts of our particular society have been weakened by incessant privation. Their restoration is a precondition for societal survival.

The first involves the fact that we have progressively instituted layers of formal regulation for government to control its citizens. This has resulted in an explosion in the direct costs of government administration. In the United States, for example, these direct costs now have reached a level of $13.2 billion in a $5 trillion economy and comprehensive regulatory costs now amount to 10% of Gross Domestic Product.[12] This process, which started in the Great Depression, has accelerated since 1960. The situation is similar in most industrial nations. At the same time that the costs of regulatory bureaucracy have mushroomed the overall standard of leadership has deteriorated. Politicians and businessmen are widely believed by the people to be rapacious and unethical. This contention is supported by mounting evidence. Citizens themselves go to great lengths to avoid requirements they dislike, such as taxes, whether or not they stay within the statutes. What we have created is an increasingly bureaucratic system inculcated with venality, rapidly losing the support of the citizens it was designed to serve.

A second area is the progressive breaking down of the continuum that once existed between living individuals and their ancestors. We seem to have forgotten that "men and women who maintain a spiritual connection with ancestors have a certain strength that may not be easily softened."[13] Sometimes it is called ethnic pride. Sometimes it is called tradition. Whatever its guise, there is an umbilical cord which can create an intangible fortitude and placidity that the technological, individualistic individuals of today seem increasingly unable to locate. Increasingly our people cannot find "the unvarying bond between themselves and their ancestral shades."[14] "When this was shattered, the land was indeed dead."[15] Our stability has been shattered both by industrial evolution and technological revolution. In the process we no longer value tradition, we no longer are connected to our ancestors. Both are too often viewed as obsolete. Only if we can repair the continuum by reinstalling humanity and humility will we be able to reassure ourselves that our land is not dead.

As newly past-connected and past-respectful groups rise into positions of influence in First World nations, unity with our past may begin to be restored. These groups include Hispanics and African-Americans in the United States, Middle Easterners in Europe, and Asians throughout. The dynamics of their influx and rediscovery could resurrect vital beliefs. Many of our collective ancestors, "did not think of the land as a resources that could be sold or otherwise disposed of, but knew they were the people who belonged to the land and were responsible to and for it."[16] It is possible that such groups could be one conduit through which the obverse of individual rights, obligations, could work their way back into the mainstream of Western society and wean us from destructive habits. If we listen to these essentially Third World voices a new Mobius Strip of lives could appear, replacing the notion that existence equals immediacy.

The final dwindling communal precept, and in many ways the most critical, is faith. Belief in something higher used to rule every life in every nation. It sometimes led to abuses. It sometimes narrowed minds. But in general it created solidity, and vitality. The seeds of its destruction may have been planted by Peter Abelard's assertion that, "I must understand in order that I may believe." The process was undoubtedly sped by the Eighteenth Century philosophical principles underlying republicanism. The arrival of the Technological Age delivered a mortal blow. For most Westerners man is now deemed the highest authority. It has become a given that he can accomplish anything. Even nature is often disregarded. This has created a void which has intensified our disorientation. Václav Havel summed up our condition. "With the loss of God, man has lost a kind of absolute and universal system of co-ordinates, to which he could always relate anything, chiefly himself. His world and his personality gradually began to break up into separate, incoherent fragments corresponding to different, relative co-ordinates. And when this happened man began to lose his inner identity, that is, his identity with himself. Along with it he lost a lot of other things too, including a sense of his own continuity, a hierarchy of experience and values, and so on. It's as if we were playing for a number of different teams at once, each with different uniforms, and as though - and this is the main thing - we didn't know which one we ultimately belonged to, which of these teams was really ours."[17]

Our civilization has been powered from its inception by the Judeo-Christian network of beliefs. For good or ill this system has been our lodestone and our engine. In recent decades it has faded from the center of our activities and with it civilization's electricity and contentment. Writer Peggy Noonan laments that, "we have lost, somehow, a sense of mystery - about us, about our purpose, our meaning, our role. Our ancestors believed in two worlds, and understood this to be the solitary, nasty, brutish, and short one. We are the first generations of man that actually expected to find happiness here on earth, and our search for it has caused such - unhappiness."[18] Whether we are the first or not is of minor significance. We must realize that following this course of belief-abandonment in a search for immediate gratification has become a primary cause of our moral decline and loss of vitality. That is the real significance for our society.

Can we reclaim the First World's precepts from bankruptcy? Certainly. It is possible to revitalize our civilization. It will take a massive effort of will to reverse recent trends and to shore up the foundation. We can re-establish extended families (even if they don't coincide with the traditional definitions). We can regain contact with our past and our beliefs. We can once again develop a sense of community. However, it will require a general agreement that this needs to be done before the coordinated effort can begin. Such an agreement is not on the horizon. Whether any reorientation materializes into an actuality will be largely determined prior to the turn of the century. By then the future course of our civilization will be set. It is already indisputable that, "The European age - the age which extended from 1648 to 1947 - is over, and with it the predominance of the old European scale of values."[19] The critical question of the next decade for our Western civilization will be whether its successor, the American age, is over as well and with it the pre-eminence of capitalistic individualism. It is still an open question. Choices still remain. But the clock is ticking.

---

1 Eugene Linden, "Megacities," *Time Magazine*, January 11, 1993, p. 31.

2 Justin Kaplan, *Lincoln Steffins* (Simon & Schuster, NY, 1974) p. 38.

3 Christopher Lasch, *The True and Only Heaven, Progress and Its Critics* (W.W. Norton & CO., 1991) p.169.

4 estimates by Tillinghast Consulting

5 Mary Ann Glendon, *Rights Talk - The Impoverishment of Political Discourse* (The Free Press, 1991) p. XI.

6 Alexis de Toqueville, *Reflections of the French Revolution of 1848* ed. J.P. Mayer and A.P. Kerr (Transaction Books, New Brunswick, NJ 1987)

p. 12.

[7] Paul Johnson, *The Birth of the Modern* (Harper Collins, 1991) p. 149.

[8] Christopher Lasch, *The True and Only Heaven* (W.W. Norton & Company, 1991) p. 169.

[9] Taylor Caldwell, *The Arm and the Darkness* (Aeonian Press, 1974) p. 329.

[10] Jay Miller, "A Kinship of Spirit," *America in 1492*, ed. Alvin M. Josephly Jr. (Alfred A. Knopf, NY, 1992) p. 326.

[11] Studs Terkel, *Race,* interview with Quinn Brisben (New Press, NY 1992) p. 183.

[12] 1992 estimates by the Center for the Study of American Business.

[13] Morley Safer, *Flashbacks on Returning to Vietnam* (Random House, NY, 1990) p. 96.

[14] Ibid.

[15] Noël Mostert, *Frontiers, The Epic of South Africa's Creation and the Tragedy of the Xhosa Peoples* (Alfred A. Knopf, NY, 1992) p.748.

[16] Robin Ridington, "Northern Hunters," *America in 1492*, ed. Alvin M. Joseph Jr. (Alfred A. Knopf, 1992) p. 33.

[17] Václav Havel, "It Always Makes Sense to Tell the Truth" an interview with Jiri Lederer, *Open Letters,* trans. Paul Wilson, April 29, 1975, (Vintage Books 1991) p. 95.

[18] Peggy Noonan, "You'd Cry Too If It Happened to You," *Forbes*, September 14, 1992, p. 65.

[19] Geoffrey Barraclough, *Introduction to Contemporary History* (Pelican Books, Middlesex, England, 1967) p. 268.

CHAPTER 5

The Future of the Republican Ideal

The 'American Dream' has served as the world's proxy for the republican ideal ever since the founding of the United States in the crucible of its war with Britain. This ideal was reflected shortly thereafter in the French Revolution, and echoed dozens of times throughout the years by those for whom it served as a model. Indeed, for this reason, the future of Western civilization depends upon the future of America. Before ascertaining what this future may be, it is necessary to briefly examine the consistency of the American Dream/republican ideal.

One of its keys has always been that "most Americans *behaved* as though they existed in a culture of equality, even though they also existed in an economy, and to a considerable extent a society, of inequality."[1] Another key as been the flexibility of the American governmental structure. Both characteristics have allowed the nation to evolve through times of immense territorial expansion, demographic change, and economic growth. The American Dream/republican ideal has sliced through repeated challenge and emerged stronger, due largely to the nature of these two fundamental characteristics - flexibility and belief in equality.

It all started in May of 1787 when the first of fifty-five eminent citizens from twelve of the original states (Rhode Island remained aloof) began to arrive in Philadelphia to attend a Constitutional Convention. They were suffering not only from the first blasts of what was to become an awesomely hot summer, but also from the effects of having spent a decade under the ineffectual aegis of the Articles of Confederation.

While this group contained some who were to become legendary historical figures, they were not all giants. They were representative of the leadership of the times. All were male. All were white. All possessed property. Most either owned slaves, or condoned the practice. The majority were Protestant, but were not deeply religious. Twenty-six had a college education.

These characteristics, along with their inherent limitations, did not prevent the men gathered in the State House from constructing a societal foundation and administrative framework that in many ways is as fresh today as it was then. How did these Eighteenth Century Founding Fathers draft a document so readily adaptable to conditions they could never have imagined?

First of all, they were able to transcend the times in which they lived and think of the future as one with the past and present. This reflected Edmund Burke's definition of society as, "a partnership, not only between those who are living, but between those who are dead and those who are to be born." The delegates exhibited this attitude, both on the convention floor and in their writing.

"To view, through the calm, sedate medium of reason, the influence which the establishment now proposed may have upon the happiness or misery of millions yet unborn is an object of such magnitude, as absorbs, and in a measure suspends, the operations of human understanding." (George Mason)

"We should consider that we are providing a Constitution for further generations." (James Wilson)

"We ought to take a permanent view of the subject and not look at the present moment only." (John Rutledge)

"The plan now being digested would decide forever the fate of republican government." (James Madison)

The result was a collective commitment to a process which would debate all issues, but produce a national statement of purpose. This statement took the form of an operable system of government containing an allocation of power which was acceptable to the majority of the country's citizens. It also included a provision for amendment. The system became known as Federalism. The nation became a republic.

Our national mission statement, our Constitution, is in effect a Social Contract. Thomas Aquinas provided its basic definition. "Government is instituted by the community and may be revoked by the community."[2] This concept was refined by the work of philosophers such as Rousseau, Locke, Hume, Hooker and Hobbes before it became imbedded in the foundation of the American community. Since that time this nation's Social Contract has never been monolithic and immutable. That is why it has survived, flourished, and shone as a beacon to others. Today it serves a nation of 250 million, over nine times the size of the original thirteen states. How well does it serve? How strong is the pulse of the United States' Social Contract?

The biggest danger the country faces is the development of alternate contracts. This periodic threat became an actuality only once, during the Civil War of 1861-1865. At other times it has responded to the inherent plasticity of the Constitution, which facilitated accommodating adjustments that allowed the threat to recede.

There is another significant threat existing in the 1990s. Its appetite is fed by the large numbers of disadvantaged and disaffected citizens whose lives seem governed by different rules than that of the majority. The core of this group is the thirty-four million persons, fourteen percent of the population, who live below the officially stated poverty line. These people, who live within the borders of the most prosperous industrial state the world has ever known, often exist under Third World conditions. They equal the population of Romania and Hungary combined or Argentina or two Malaysias. The thirty-four million include a preponderance of children, single parents, and non-whites. Virtually all must attend substandard educational facilities, live in dilapidated housing, and go about their daily activities surrounded by violence and crime. They feel disenfranchised, deprived of respect for their own existence, and shorn of any prospects for sharing the American Dream. Most ominously, they also feel that they have little to lose. Like Robert Rocha they have felt, "there was no way I could trust anybody with my feelings. Nobody had ever cared about me, so why should I care about anyone else."[3]

Historically the most deprived members of a community by themselves have rarely been the catalyst for major change. Thus, the development of three specific demographic conditions could prove crucial to the outlook for Social Contract unity in the Twenty-First Century.

Fifty years ago Americans of European descent accounted for eighty percent of the population. Fifty years from now they will comprise twenty-five percent to thirty percent. White males, who since the nation's founding have controlled most of the governmental, industrial, educational, and eleemosynary instruments of power, account for thirty percent of the population today. That percentage will progressively decline. The two fastest growing age groups in the United States over the next fifty years will be those over 65 and those under 18. Most of the 32 million people now over 65 are white. Most of the 65 million under 18 years old are Afro-Americans and Hispanics. The United States government annually spends $11,000 on every person over 65 and $4,200 on ever person under 18. The older group accounts for 13% of the population and receives 29% of all Federal outlays. The youths account for 26% of the population and receive only 7% of all Federal monies.

Whether America confronts these disparities, and how it attempts to deal with them, will heavily influence the course of its Contract. Collectively the social, economic, and political alterations necessary to surmount these challenges will be as great as any nation has ever effected.

The republican simplicity of Jefferson and Madison has become obfuscated in the process of government. "In 1815 the President paid, out of his own pocket, the single secretary who assisted him; the Supreme Court convened for two months a year in a Capital Hill boarding house."[4] Even by 1829 the entire United States Federal Government (excluding Congress and the Military) for a population of 12.5 million people consisted of 352 individuals. That was one Federal official for every 37,000 people. In 1992 there were 37,000 functionaries employed by the two houses of Congress alone, which created over 300 committees and subcommittees to occupy them. This provides 69 staffers for each legislator and one staffer for every 7,000 citizens. Also in 1992 there were 33,704 lobbyists registered just with the United States Senate. This was 337 lobbyists for each Senator and one per 7,000 citizens. Government at all levels employs 18.6 million people, one for every 17 citizens. The cost of providing governmental regulation is over $500 billion, more than 10% of Gross Domestic Product. Collectively these numbers suggest that the growth and complexity of government has far outpaced that of society. Both Federalism and republicanism have been buried under a bureaucratic avalanche.

In the early 1990s the United States faces a watershed period of choices. A multiplicity of problems bombards its inhabitants daily, both through the media and their own observation. A majority of Americans believe that their grandchildren will have less prosperous and less satisfactory lives than their own. The gap between the most advantaged and the most disadvantaged citizens has increased for over a decade, making any pretense of equality more difficult. The pivotal middle class is seeing its American Dream slip away. As its income and prospects dwindle its optimism has diminished concomitantly.

These problems have been exacerbated by self-interest and special interests, which seem poised to rip the nation asunder. The United States can revive its republican ideal only if it can realize that, "in order for a community to progress and thrive its members must recognize the requirements of the total community and temper their individual behavior within the framework of those requirements."[5] To a large extent the future of Western civilization hinges upon this realization and upon the attendant adjustments.

History will render the verdict. For this verdict to be positive United States citizens should heed Andrew Jackson's advice. "The rich and powerful too often bend the acts of government to their selfish purposes...By attempting to gratify their desires we have in the results of our legislation arrayed section against section, interest against interest, and man against man, in a fearful commotion which threatens to shake the foundation of our Union...The humble members of our society who have neither the time nor the means of securing like favors to themselves have a right to complain of the injustice of their government."[6] Will the nation empower its ordinary citizens? Will these citizens respond? Answers to these two questions could prove pivotal to the American age.

Alarms have periodically sounded throughout the history of the United States. Each time the overwhelming popular response has been an attempt to rectify and a compulsion to evolve. This time the fate of all Western civilization will likely depend upon achieving such a response. Each year that passes with only token gestures towards defusing the threats to the American Dream/republican ideal makes the required task greater and the ultimate outlook murkier.

---

1 James MacGregor Burns, *The Vineyard of Liberty* (Alfred A. Knopf, NY 1982) p. 356.

2 De Regime Principium

3 Hank Whittemore's interview with Dr. Mimi Silbert, *Parade Magazine* March 15, 1992.

4 Charles Sellars, T*he Market Revolution* (Oxford University Press, NY, 1991) p. 37.

5 Emmett C. Murphy with Michael Snell, *The Genius of Sitting Bull* (Prentice Hall, 1992) p. 28.

6 Andrew Jackson, Veto of the Recharter of the Second Bank of the United States, July 10, 1832

PART II

The Temporary Rise of Spherism

"What I see in the World today is not a growing sense of interdependence, but, on the contrary, a growing withdrawal into isolation or rival blocs."

Geoffrey Barraclough
"Planning for a New Economic Order"
New York Review of Books August 1975

CHAPTER 6

Atrophy of Internationalism: Growth of Super Spheres

The world is currently coagulating into a kaleidoscope of protected regions. The era of internationalism, to the extent that it existed in the 1970s and 1980s, is gradually disappearing behind the walls being erected to guard purportedly essential industries and services from each other's incursions.

It is true that the Soviet Bloc, and with it COMECON[1], has dissolved. The final years of its demise seemed to bring a last flash of freely flowing commerce as fresh trading ground was assayed by the West and new turf-lines drawn. This process, though still in a state of flux, is largely complete.

What is emerging from the detritus of COMECON and the skeletal foundation of GATT[2] is an interlocking pattern of Influence Spheres, only fluid around their edges. At the moment these spheres are anchored by the United States, Germany, and Japan. Two others are nascent, and as the next century approaches may coalesce around the cores of China and Fundamental Islam. The latter could flourish strongly in more than one guise, in more than one location. This pattern is fragile, though. It could succumb to the stress of warfare, either military or economic. It could also shatter under the pressure of civilization's transmogrification. For the time being, spherism is in place, and is slowly oozing throughout the globe.

THE FACT OF SPHERES

Influence Spheres have existed since the earliest days of prehistory. They started as trading centers, were often enhanced by colonies, and sometimes evolved into empires. The scope of influence widened as transportation improved, such as when the Cretans learned to conquer the sea, or when rail lines stretched their iron tentacles.

At times spheres have seemed almost unitary, as with the Pax Romana of the Second Century or the Mongol Empire of the Thirteenth. At other times there has been more of a bifurcation. This was the case when the Axis confronted the Allies in World War II, or when Communism faced off against Democracy in the cold war thereafter. The most frequent occurrence is some form of multiplicity. It was dramatically exemplified by the world-wide race to stake out territorial and commercial claims among the several powers of the late Nineteenth Century.

In the post-World War II years the globe has been exposed to an alphabet soup of organizations, alliances, and associations including NATO, ASEAN, OAS, EFTA and the OECD[3]. Perhaps the most enduring and influential have been the EEC and OPEC[4], with the others drifting in between strong cooperation to meet a specific threat and loose confederation meeting to draft innocuous resolutions.

OPEC continues despite many conflicts among its members. It maintains the latent ability, unsheathed only occasionally, to bring the industrial economies to their knees. The EEC is a different story. Founded in 1957 largely through the efforts of Frenchmen, Jean Monnet and Robert Schuman, as well as Belgian Paul Henry Spaak, it originally included six nations which had the aim of gradually lowering economic and political barriers, thus creating greater unity and power for Europe. Its high water mark (as the newly-christened European Community) occurred in December 1991 with the signing of the 250 page Maastricht Treaty by twelve nations. They pledged to create, along with a single currency and one central bank, commonly administered policies for economics, foreign policy, and defense. They also agreed to accept new members. This treaty has yet to be unanimously ratified, as required, and is undergoing several court challenges, but ultimate enactment seems likely. However, it is much less likely that the EC will ever function as intended.

So the world sits in 1993 with no COMECON a stillborn EC, a gestating NAFTA[5] and a GATT[6] perilously close to unraveling.

Recession has spread over Europe, North America, and Japan. All industrial nations are looking to stimulate their economies, safeguard their industries, and reduce levels of unemployment. The gravitation towards spherism has begun. Its shape is emerging from the shadows.

THE REASONS FOR FORMATION

The impetus to form protective structures is simple. Basically, the rigors of competition become too severe. First World elements, such as farmers in France or steel producers in the United States, deem themselves unable to survive without pleading to their governments for subsidies or tariffs. The trauma of facing obsolescence, retraining, and relocation proves too great. Despite what politicians and economists say, if inhabitants of the Industrial World ask themselves: Do we really have a free market? or, Do we really want a free market? The answer is usually a resounding no, or at best a qualified yes. Many are afraid of real competition. Most advocate the principle that the engine of Industrial World production should maintain its collective dominance, and are fundamentally fearful over the possible impact of freer trade on specific national industries. Gunnar Myrdal noticed these tendencies. "The share in world trade of the non-industrial nations, which contain over three-quarters of the world's population, is lower than in 1928, when they were still undeveloped, and the average standard of living of humanity as a whole is still below the level of 1900. Everywhere, in short, the law of cumulative inequality is at work, creating discrepancies more glaring than in the past." This condition has made negotiation between the 'haves' and 'have-nots' more difficult and intensified the shock waves as multinational corporations shifted production from one low cost Third World site to another. Despite political rhetoric, the current global situation is not creating lower trade barriers and greater international economic cooperation. It is not generating greater equality or raising the overall standard of living. It actually is fostering the reverse. Why is this so?

One reason is that there are a plethora of variables running amok, outside effective regional or international control. These include gyrating currencies, instantly responsive financial markets, embedded unemployment, expanding environmental pollution, and demands for industrial safety. Exacerbating these variables are uneven rates of productivity and the constant labor-management tug-of-war over work rules. A further factor is the establishment of moneyed elites as nations industrialize, widening the gap between them and the less fortunate, but skewing statistical averages. All of these conspire to create a sense of insecurity among even the most advanced industrial technological nations. Questions of what can be done to protect the environment from acid rain or to hedge against strength in the Japanese yen, become issues of policy with sectors ranged against each other and the largely unregulated multinational corporations trying to operate in-between. This competition has encouraged the various Industrial World constituencies, looking at threats, real or perceived, to huddle increasingly with those who suffer similarly instead of attempting to bridge those ever-widening gaps. Consistently their reactions are ones of nations which, "are faced with the task of defending a high standard of living and all the luxuries of a permissive society against the jealousies...of countless millions who are just awakening to an awareness of world affairs, and who would witness without pity or regret the disappearance of much that we value."[7] The actual policies of the various industrial/technological nations are developing into attempts to protect an imagined status quo rather than to form wider swaths of cooperation. This sentiment is intensified by events, such as cross border take-over raids, or conflicting understanding of fundamental concepts, such as environmental protection.

The Industrial World stands today with its policies progressively leaning away from internationalism and towards regionalism. At the same time its efforts to organize transnationally are stuttering. Negotiations to strengthen GATT are bogged down. The EC's formation is behind schedule and it may emerge as a cipher of its intention. The methodology of NAFTA's enactment is being disputed. Asia has yet to support any multinational association in a meaningful manner. Spherism continues to take shape, gathering strength from fears and insecurities.

THE PROCESS OF FORMATION

In the 1970s and 1980s the industrial nations, to some extent, opened up economically to welcome internationalism. Currency agreements were concluded, tariff barriers were lowered, travel restrictions were reduced, sophisticated communication links were established, and multinational corporations were unleashed to roam the world for markets and production sites. Then a series of circumstances began to hamper this effort and cause the erstwhile internationalists to recoil.

The first was the oil embargo by OPEC in 1974. The embargo highlighted the industrial nations' dependence upon fuel, especially upon fuel from outside sources. It initially fostered programs of self-sufficiency, conservation, pressure to conclude bilateral agreements with producing nations, and a painful realization of the costs required to defend Middle East oil fields from hostile incursion. Initially it seemed as if long lines at the fuel pump had riveted citizens' focus on the international aspects of their daily lives. But gradually efforts at self-sufficiency and conservation degenerated into a general energy policy, that culminated in the Gulf War of 1991. The policy involved protecting low cost crude oil sources. Under the surface the cumulative industrial citizenry refused to change their life styles. There was no real re-ordering of priorities. There was no willingness to curb national consumption. These tendencies spread over areas other than energy. Rather than self-discipline there was concern about issues such as job losses, domestic market shares of foreign products, the need to create a 'level playing field' and attempted curtailment for foreign ownership of indigenous assets. Campaigns to 'Buy America' were symptomatic. Recessions, trade deficits, and other economic difficulties have served to hone the blade of reaction and protection, cutting through the veneer of free trade and free markets.

As the 1980s unfolded the long-promised EC took a more formal shape. Concomitantly, one of its chief objectives become not only to create a large single market, but to protect it. This sentiment applied to a wide range of activities from financial services, to automobile manufacture, to farming. Companies flocked to Europe from overseas to establish bases for participation while the opportunity existed. This flood in and of itself created resentment and boosted efforts to forestall the internationalization process.

The United States, under the Bush Administration, assumed an aggressive trade stance against exporting nations, particularly Japan, who were repeatedly accused of unfair competition. This aggressiveness has by and large continued under President Clinton. Environmental cooperation has buckled under pressure from American business which resists any attempt to externally dictate its industrial practices. The United States' fast-track trade policy emphasis shifted from formulation of an operable GATT to putting NAFTA together. However, fearing job losses and lack of environmental control, among other things, businesses, unions, and consumers have diluted the impact of even this regional proposal. The operation of NAFTA has became threatened. The immediate reaction of the First World to any agreement or proposal transcending national borders, whether it be commercial, political, or military, is the type of defensive reaction associated with nations protecting dwindling assets rather than the confidence of societies in expansion

In short, the concentration of the industrial nations has shifted. They are searching for ways to insulate, narrow their scope, withdraw from entanglements. Spheres of influence and activity are being slowly constructed around the national interests of the selected core members, and should gradually widen .

THE RAMIFICATIONS OF FORMATION

Milton Friedman has lamented an opportunity lost. "There may be half a billion to a billion potential workers in China, Eastern Europe, and Latin America. And that constitutes a real revolution in possible cooperation between capital-rich countries. It could give us the equivalent of another Industrial Revolution. But what bothers me is this: Not only the United States but other countries seem to be missing this enormous opportunity. The capital-rich countries are going in a protectionist direction, building walls around their blocs; Fortress Europe, the United States with Canada and Mexico."[8] The opportunity for this revolution will not be seized as strongly as it might have been. Cooperation between capital and labor pools may not be on a world scale. However, it will take place regionally. The impetus will come from an attempt to stave off the adverse effects of demographics on the work force, on production, and on consumer purchasing proclivities, as well as from an attempt to secure important natural resources.

The United States is an excellent example of the demographic impetus. Its number of 25-year-olds will increase steadily from October 1993 to March 1996. Every new household formed by a 25-year-old adds about $12,000 to Gross Domestic Product in the form of new consumer spending, mostly on durables. By 1996 the baby boom generation (the 77 million born between 1946 and 1964) will start to turn 55. This is an age when consumer spending begins to decline. By then there will be more boomers turning 55 than young people turning 25, putting downward pressure on spending. New consumers will be needed to take up the fruits of industrial production as well as to make up the labor force.

By the second decade of the next century there will be only two United States workers earning the money to sustain each over-65 year old receiving 'Entitlement'[9] funds. This is a decline from the four workers supporting each senior in 1992. These trends highlight the dire financial need for a fresh approach to the way the labor force, the market place, and production are regarded. One way to accomplish that is through some sort of regional cooperation, like NAFTA. Without debating such controversial issues, such as whether a NAFTA-type association will or won't cost the United States jobs near its border with Mexico, or whether it will intensify problems in the areas of monitoring worker safety and the environment, it is possible to delineate several important national goals that will surely be served from this type of spheric regionalism.

First is the fact that the significant energy resources of Mexico and Canada can increase the United States' prospects for self-sufficiency. It could create an energy self-sufficient region which is both highly industrialized and amply supplied with natural resources. No other area of the world is in a position to do this.

Second, the population of Mexico (at 88 million) is roughly triple the size of California, promising both wider markets and a source of less expensive, motivated labor. In 1992 an average Mexican consumed $380 worth of United States' products per year, which is $20 more than the average South Korean buys. Mexicans do this on an average annual income that is less than half that of the average South Korean. The Mexican Gross Domestic Product per capita has risen sharply in recent years, and is now over $3,400, the level of the more prosperous Eastern Europeans. In 1991 the United States, for the first time in a decade, had a merchandise trade surplus with Mexico (even though 85% of Mexican merchandise exports are to the United States). That surplus grew to $5.5 billion in 1992.

Third, "nearly four out of ten 18-year-olds entering the continental labor force are Mexicans - this in a country with a mere 5% of United States gross national product ($334 billion vs. $6 trillion)."[10] Resources, markets, labor supply all make Mexico important to the future of the United States. Canada provides the additional plusses of a developed nation with abundant natural resources and miles of empty territory.

Finally, even if NAFTA eventually extends no further south than Mexico, the cultural synergy with the United States' 25 million resident Hispanic-Americans (plus an estimated 2 million illegal Mexican immigrants) is evident. All of these factors will make the transition from internationalism to regionalism seem less ominous, and make it increasingly likely. Regional production and politics will progressively grow less confusing and more comfortable. This will happen elsewhere also. Regional Influence Spheres will progressively work their way into the cultural ethic of Industrial World nations, most of whom will perceive themselves in an escalating struggle against other areas of the world for the survival of their accustomed way of life.

Such a sequence will take place in North America. It will take place in Europe. It may take place in East Asia. These regions will continue to turn inward. They will concentrate on industrialization. They will emphasis market development, particularly of the weaker elements within their regions. They will focus on those issues that can be defined regionally. They will attempt to filter out exogenous turmoil. They will husband their assets, and fortify their barriers. In the process of so doing all of these spheres will be subject to extraordinary tensions.

---

[1] Council for Mutual Economic Assistance

[2] General Agreement on Tariffs and Trade

[3] North American Treaty Organization, Association of South East Asian Nations, Organization of American States, European Free Trade Association, and Organization for Economic Cooperation and Development

[4] European Economic Community and Organization of Petroleum Exporting Countries

[5] North American Free Trade Association proposed to include Canada, the United States, and Mexico.

[6] General Agreement on Tariffs and Trade

[7] George Kennan, *Russia, the Atom and the West* (Harper & Bros., NY 1957) p. 112.

[8] Milton Friedman, *Forbes*, May 17, 1992

[9] those monies, such as Social Security and Medicare, to which citizen as are entitled by law

[10] Stephen Baker, Geri Smith, Elizabeth Weiner, "The Mexican Worker," *Business Week*, April 19, 1993, p. 86.

CHAPTER 7

Spherical Tensions

The world faces an imminent onslaught from the Four Horsemen of the Apocalypse.[1] As this onslaught intensifies the industrial nations will continue their retreat into protected Influence Spheres. The tensions of the modern world, crackling through their rarefied atmospheres, will serve to focus the minds of inhabitants on the survival of their own particular way of life. These life styles will be threatened by at least seven identifiable areas of spherical tension, currently in their adolescent stages. All promise to partition the world into inward facing spheres laden with social paranoia and anxiously peering over their battlements at hordes of 'have not' predators waiting to consume their assets.

MIGRATIONS

Paul Kennedy in his book, "Preparing for the Twenty-First Century"[2] enumerated the massive demographic pressures confronting today's world. Fernand Braudel focused on a century from the past. "Any large population increasement must occur simultaneously throughout entire humanity. The Sixteenth Century, then, must have been one of these periods of general demographic advance...This increase was universal, (in) that it was common to both rich regions and poor, to the population of the plains, the mountains, and the steppes, to all towns, whatever their size, and all rural districts... This biological revolution was the major factor in all the other revolutions with which we are concerned...This increase lay behind all the triumphs and catastrophes of a century during which man was first a useful worker and then, as the century wore on, a growing burden. By 1550 the turning point had been reached. There were too many people for comfort. Towards 1600 this overload halted expansion in new directions and with the rise of banditry, the latent social crises whose effects were felt everywhere, prepared the way for the bitter awakenings of the Seventeenth Century."[3] Vast migrations occurred, both within Europe and overseas. "Uprisings, riots and disturbances, the alarming spread of vagabonds and vagrants, increasing attacks by bandits, the sounds of violence, although frequently muffled, all tell us something about the extraordinary rise of poverty towards the end of the Sixteenth Century."[4] "Soon the problem of the poor had progressed beyond the narrow confines of the unsympathetic towns, reaching nation-wide and European dimensions...Even in Turkey the trend was towards the pauperization of considerable masses of people in desperate need of daily bread."[5] History is replete with similar examples. Is this what historians will write about the end of the Twentieth Century? It is possible. The demographic pressures are there.

The United Nations estimates that there are over 100 million people in the world who are homeless, destitute and deprived. Over 18 million have had their homes destroyed. An average of 10,000 refugees a day flee their homelands. Most of these are in the Third World. Approximately one billion of the world's population of slightly over five billion live below the poverty level established by the World Bank.[6] As is suggested in *East West Migrations*[7] the majority who roam between nations are seeking employment opportunities. They do not willingly choose idleness. "People who do emigrate are self-selected - the most ambitions, enterprising, energetic, enthusiastic, adaptable and persevering of the working and middle class."[8] The evidence, from most economists who study the situation, is that migrations theoretically could fulfill Milton Friedman's expectations. They could offset the shrinkage in the industrial nations' labor force as they have done, for example, in Japan or Western Europe. In the United States there were 8.7 million legal immigrants (plus an estimated 2 million illegals) in the 1980s which equaled the previous record decade of 1900 through 1910. This occurred while both productivity and jobs were rising. These immigrants did not detract materially from the quality of the work force, since 1.5 million were college educated and many others possessed technical skills.

However, people in the industrial countries are growing less positive about these migrations. A 1992 *Business Week* / Harris poll showed that 68% of the American public thought immigration would be bad, now and in the future, although it had been good in the past. This was a typical reaction. Industrial nations even now see the spectre of multitudes poised to overrun their territory. Nowhere is this more evident than in Western Europe. Projections of an assault by 10 to 20 million refugees[9] have proliferated, frightening Europeans and sending them scrambling to shut their borders. Austria has 2,000 troops patrolling its 204 mile frontier with Hungary. Germany is balking at any increase of its 1.5 million immigrants (7% of the population). Spain and Italy have seen 500,000 North Africans enter illegally over the last five years, and fear the influx of more. The former Yugoslavia has spewed forth 620,000 refugees since 1990, and the number is escalating daily. Wary eyes from everywhere in Europe are cast towards Russia, Eastern Europe, and the Middle East.

The several spheres are poised to slam the gates. They are no longer turning outward, encouraging immigration. They are growing hostile, listening to rightist politicians, cringing at the possibility of further arrivals. As the demographic explosion in the Third World continues the pressure will grow to build the walls higher and thicker.

DISEASE

The bubonic plague, the Black Death, came out of Central Asia or India (accounts vary) and struck continental Europe in 1342. It hit England in 1349. Subsequent waves came in 1361, 1368, 1375, and finally 1665. This disease wiped out at least one third of Europe in the Fourteenth Century, with many cities suffering over 50 percent casualties. England is a good example of what happened. "Apart from the catastrophic mortality of 1349 itself, the plague caused a long decline in population. England in the reign of Edward II was a heavily populated country in which cultivable land was scarce. In the Fifteenth Century it was quite different. We do not know exactly how much of this change was due to the plague; the great floods and famines of the years 1315-17 had perhaps been the turning point which ended the medieval expansion of population. In the over-populated England of 1315 many people must have lived on plots of land which could barely support them, or on barely adequate wages, so that they were very vulnerable to any natural calamity. Population growth may have been halted by the natural limits of subsistence. But there is little doubt that the plague was the main factor in causing a steep fall of population...It is quite likely that a population of about 3.5 millions[10] in the early Fourteenth Century had been reduced to 2.5 millions by the sudden and then gradual fall lasting into the mid-Fifteenth Century...It was probably not before the reign of Elizabeth I that as many people lived in England as had done in the reign of Edward II."[11] The last recorded major instance of Bubonic Plague was in China's Hunan province in 1865, but it still exists today, in Africa and incubating among the marmosets of Mongolia.

In this and countless other instances throughout history, nature via disease winnowed over-crowded areas, reducing demographic pressure. While unfortunate for the poor victims, this process was not necessarily a setback for society. "It would be a great mistake to suppose that English society was quickly crushed by this series of disasters. On the contrary there are many reasons for thinking that in the reign of Richard II (1377-99) it blossomed in a profusion of original activity such as it had never known before."[12] Disease has been one of nature's regulatory devices, helping to adjust the population setting so that resources and people were better balanced.

At present we live in an era that emphasizes technology. Advances in medical science have cured or curtailed many existing diseases and lowered death rates, dramatically increasing the population growth in many areas. In the Industrial World we steadfastly profess to believe that a cure for any ailment can be found. However, this has not always transpired. Millions still die from cancer and heart disease, old killers. Supposedly conquered illnesses, such as measles, cholera, and malaria, are recurring with a vengeance, especially in the urban environments of the less developed nations. New, more virulent strains of known diseases are appearing, exemplified by Yellow Fever, influenza and tuberculosis. Maladies with no known cures periodically raise their heads, such as Lyme Disease, Legionnaires' Disease, Epstein-Barr Syndrome and Hepatitis B.

Then there is AIDS[13]. There is as yet no known cure or even an effective palliative. Often the incubation period is seven or eight years. It is passed from person to person, presumably through body fluids. The World Health Organization estimates that by the year 2000 at least 40 million people will be infected with HIV[14] (versus 11-12 million in 1992). Over 90% of those infected will be in the Third World. There were 1.5 million actual AIDS cases in 1990. The estimate is that there will be a minimum of 18-20 million cases in the year 2000. The disease will have orphaned over 10 million children by the decade's end. The hardest hit area will be Black

Africa, with some estimates running as high as 50 percent of the population being infected by the end of the century. Regions such as Eastern Asia and Latin America, which thought themselves to have low levels of risk, find an epidemic on their hands. AIDS has already caused significant behavioral changes within the industrialized countries. More changes will come. Also destabilizing will be the fear of losing medical control while being inundated by infected immigrants. Regulations will tighten, as will borders. This is but one international disease. The physical and psychological reverberations are not yet of Black Death proportions, but are moving in that direction.

The fact is that modern medicine has not solved all the viral puzzles. Microbes that have existed on earth for millions of years are adapting, mutating, spreading, insulating themselves from the latest research products. There are innumerable tropical viruses, such as dengue fever, waiting for the proper catalyst. The biggest boost to contagion will come from the spreading mass of fetid urbanization, particularly in the Third World. The evidence suggests that, contrary to technological aspirations, disease and its close relative, starvation, will wreak their customary havoc. Along with warfare and natural disasters these will serve once again to temper the rush of demography and stave off a Malthusian cataclysm.

A key question is how will the First World react? How long will our sympathy last? How far can we sustain a belief in the ultimate triumph of medicine? When will we perceive the global and regional threat of burgeoning disease ridden populations and retreat behind spherical borders, guarding whatever remedies exist?

It is most likely that before being fully able to challenge the First World and its satellite Influence Spheres, populations in the Third World will be radically pruned by disease, military actions, and natural disasters. It is also likely that the First World will increasingly be a behind-the-barricade observer to this suffering, shunning the hazardous and expensive trenches.

THE ENVIRONMENT

The possibility of Global Warming and concomitant ozone layer depletion has galvanized world attention on the environment arousing preservational passion in more than just Rachel Carsonites. In the industrial nations there are two extremes. There are both 'greens' and proponents of 'progress'. The former point to the massive industrial pollution that has poisoned air, contaminated water, and, through toxic waste, infected the earth itself. They advocate an end to virtually all industrial development. The latter chafe at regulations which raise costs and impede development. They advocate a lowering of regulatory barriers and exercising control by enacting measures such as Third World population control and creation of a free market in pollution credits. The debate is full of heat and laced with facts and experts supporting both sides. The majority of people contain elements of both extremes in varying proportions.

In the developing world there are also two extremes. One yearns for the advancements and life styles of the technological era. It takes advantage of generally lax supervision to accelerate the process of industrialization. At the other extreme are the tribal societies, revering the customs of their past. They bridle at any attempt to modernize and thus dissolve all that they have held sacred. The first group, backed by the Industrial World, has had more influence and as a result vast areas have been ravaged. Rain forests have been devastated in places like Brazil, and Borneo, pandering both to the demands of settlers and to a hunger for exports. Their attitude is expressed by the governor of Brazil's Amazonas province, Gilberto Mestrinho Reposa de Medeiros. "We can't be condemned to external misery because some nutty ecologists insist that Amazonia remain untouchable."[15] Removal of vegetation has caused droughts to be exacerbated and deserts to be expanded. Fertility is being turned into fragility by overuse.

In a general way the battle lines have been drawn between the two worlds. While most First Worlders advocate modest controls on industries at home, looking South they advocate population control and limitations on local manufacturing. This delivers a body blow to those in developing areas who see any opportunity to emulate the prosperous Northern Hemisphere slipping away. On the other hand, Third Worlders also resent population control measures, which often interfere with religious beliefs or family traditions or even existence and are viewed as blatant discrimination. First World 'progress' advocates react adversely to Third World suggestions that industrial regulations be tightened, calling them hypocritical threats to domestic profits, jobs, and market shares. The only roads to compromise appear to be on a regional level, as less developed areas are selectively included in Influence Spheres to provide market outlets, labor supplies, and valuable resources.

It is incontrovertible that there is no known way to transform the Third World into a clone of the First without facing environmental catastrophe. Given population growth trends the world's present 5 billion people will increase to 9 billion in the first quarter of the next century, with the majority living in Third World urban areas. Raising levels of consumption without a corresponding geometric leap in pollution control technology and funding would court environmental instability. This prospect will force the industrial spheres, attended by their developing world cohorts, to turn ever more inward. They will become stingier both in promoting growth elsewhere and in sharing both the technology and the resources under their control.

CONTROL OF SCARCE RESOURCES

An extension of the environmental conundrum is the one involving resources. The United States, for example, has 4% of the world's population, but it consumes one quarter of the world's oil production. The resource appetite of the Industrial World is voracious. It is possible that in the future there will be revolutionary technological developments that will conserve some of the resource base. At the moment there is nothing on the horizon that is promising to do more than dent the problem.

Resources have always been critical to the development of civilizations. The Roman Empire expanded to secure agricultural supplies and minerals. The British Imperial span was in a large part based upon acquisition of resources to power the Industrial Revolution. Prior to World War II the Japanese Greater East Asia Co-Prosperity Sphere had as its primary purpose the funneling of raw materials into a growing industrial and military machine. The recent Gulf War was joined by a United States-led United Nations to protect, for the industrial nations, the Arabian Peninsula's vital reserves of oil.

The first great multinational corporations were resource oriented: oil, timber, minerals, agriculture. Now most multinational corporations are industrial and consumer based. Their future incremental growth depends largely upon the industrialization and consumerization of the Third World. Since the Third World contains most of the available natural resources the battle over their control, to say nothing of their right to industrialize, will be critical to First World corporate profits.

Peruvian theologist Gustavo Guiterrez put the situation neatly. "Liberation theology demands that the present exploitation of four-fifths of the human family by the remaining one-fifth be ended through rapid social change. It holds that whether this change comes violently of non-violently depends on the actions of the minority rather than the majority, but either way it will come." It has come. Middle East oil producers are building petrochemical plants, obsoleting many in the First World. Technology centers, mini-Silicon Valleys, have sprouted among the maquilladoras on the Mexican side of the Rio Grande; in Panang, Malaysia, and on the island of Singapore. Steel mills, auto plants, toy factories, and assembly lines for cookies all dot the landscape of previously undeveloped countries. These countries are increasingly producing in partnership with, or even independent of, the Industrial World's multinationals. They are already looking to protect their inherent resources, and their growing markets, while their erstwhile partners grow more insistent about filling their own needs for both goods and cash flow.

If Third World economies expand, as First World policies are encouraging them to do, who will have title to what's in the ground, as well as the goods and services produced on top of it? The signs are that it will be increasingly difficult for this control to remain with the industrialized nations and their multinational minions. Developing countries from China to Mexico are already demanding larger equity slices in, and often absolute sovereignty over, vital resources such as energy. To what degree is the First World prepared for more economic sanctions and military action? To what degree can it afford them?

There is a likely alternative. The industrial powers can organize spheres of influence that are as self-sufficient as possible, and defend them tenaciously. The United States is in by far the best position to do this. Its region is a vast market place, amply stocked with resources, facing few border threats. Its main challenges are to preserve its own unity and stem its profligacy. The other industrial centers, Germany and Japan are far less well situated. Both lie amid fragmented markets, with a dearth of resources and several strong border threats. Japan in particular will soon find itself struggling for its own survival under the looming economic and military might of China. Its closest customers and suppliers may be impeded by recurring warfare. Its network of overseas production will be vulnerable to interdiction. With escalating military needs, an aging labor force, greater strains on its financial resources, and dependence on a far flung manufacturing complex, Japan will be under intense pressure.

Bitter conflicts are erupting over the right to act as chatelaine of scarce resources, economic and political volatility has increased. Throughout the world both national and corporate financial health have deteriorated. Shortages persist. 'Have not' areas have tended to grow relatively poorer and more exploited. As a result internationalism is on the wane, protection is rising, and large scale armed conflict did not die with the Cold War. Resources will be at the heart of this process as they have been so often in the past.

RISING MILITARISM

From the Bosphorus to the Sea of Okhotsk, Asia is becoming an armed camp. It is engaged in a deadly race to expand and modernize its military forces. The major battles of the next fifty years are likely to take place within, or adjacent, to its borders. Some of them will utilize nuclear weapons, at least of a tactical nature, as Asia now contains seven actual or potential nuclear powers.[16] Four nations: China;India; Russia and North Korea each have over one million persons in their military. Defense spending is rising across the continent. Japan with the region's most modern armed forces, "by some measures...now spends more on defense than any other country but America"[17], and its spending, as a percent of Gross Domestic Product, is rising. "Asia's powers, mindful of history, both ancient and modern, think that, despite the present lack of tension, almost any one of them could quickly become an outright enemy of any of the others."[18]

As Europe and the United States wind down their military machines and involvements, Asia is going in the opposite direction. A major question for the next twenty or thirty years will be the extent to which non-Asian industrial nations will become involved in Asian conflicts. Japan will perforce be involved. Will Germany the United States and the rest of Europe be able to stay on the sidelines watching the destruction behind a moated abatis of indifference? The answer to this question will determine both the quality and the duration of their life styles. It will also determine the nature and timing of the next civilization.

"Asia's balance of power is both complex and delicate. Only one Pacific power - the United States - has the resources, the impartiality, the trust of enough Asian countries and the self-interest to keep the region from toppling into instability."[19] It is increasingly unlikely that the United States will be willing to become involved in Asia as it focuses on problems within its home region. Thus, it will not be a convenient arbiter, and Asia's maelstrom will swirl unchecked by the West.

There are two distinct parts to Asia, and its militarism. They are defined primarily by geography. The first is East Asia with its high economic growth, swatches of industrial sophistication, and centuries of bitter rivalries. "If Europe continues to slash arms spending and Asian trends continue, East Asia will be the world's most heavily armed by the century's end."[20] "It is the emphasis on technology imports that sets the East Asian races apart from those in the Third World."[21] At issue will be access to resources, control over sources of industrial production, and, maybe most important of all, acquisition of territory to house mushrooming populations. The main contestants will be China, Japan, and India.

West Asia, which contains most of the Middle East as well as elements of the former Soviet Union, is not likely to be a sea of tranquillity either. It too has ancient antagonisms. But most of all it sits on vast lakes of oil. West Asia's overriding problem will be the shock waves from Fundamental Islam's drive to take over oil fields and acquire religious leadership. Across the Asian continent conflict will be continuous and destructive with alliances forming and dissolving, and nations appearing and disappearing. This situation is likely to persist at least through the first quarter of the coming century.

The demands and consequences of militarism will derail Japan's current East Asian economic hegemony[22] and delay China's accession. They will embroil both flourishing[23] and incipient[24] economic tigers, as well as hosts of others, in activities very different from those in which they excelled in the 1980s and early 1990s. "What makes the situation in the regions so significant, however, is the combination of growing economic resources with which to pursue these plans and the emergence in many of these countries of civilian industries with considerable scientific and technological expertise."[25] Militarism will also create two conditions for Western Influence Spheres. First, it will pose a challenge - how much involvement? Second, it will grant a possible respite due to less outside economic pressure. In any event it will eventually remove important production and resources, possibly including the Middle East oil fields, from Western control.

RELIGION

Historically the greatest element of stress in the world has been provided by religion. Some postulate that changes in industrial society have made widespread religious tension unlikely in the next few decades. Since the Fifteenth Century the driving force of Western Civilization has grown gradually less intensely religious. At the same time it has become more materialistic. One result of this trend has led to quests, such as the one articulated by Stephan Hawking. "If we do discover a complete theory (of the universe), it should in time be understandable in broad principle by everyone, not just a few scientists. Then we shall all, philosophers, scientists, and just ordinary people, be able to take part in the discussion of the question of why it is that we and the universe exist. If we find the answer to that, it would be the ultimate triumph of human reason - for then we would know the mind of God."[26] The triumph of rational man, the religion of the technological age, that is what Hawking is describing. He is echoing a certain element at the cutting edge of industrial society that strives to demystify even the deepest secrets. "Science and religion, after almost four centuries of conflict, had arrived at a modus vivendi; Science did one thing, religion did another: there was no logical contradiction, but to Professor Weinberg[27] and others there clearly is: physics seem capable of invading - and supplanting - the realms of religion and philosophy."[28] For these people more than the world's mechanism can be revealed by science. They infer that components of belief can be quantified. Their purpose seems directed to make unquestionable faith a waning force, to dissolve the mists of mystery. For them technology is providing moral structure.

But for increasing numbers of the Industrial World's citizens the technological system is not working. Their lives are not rewarding, their values have slipped away. A series of polls conducted in the United States and elsewhere have uncovered large numbers of individuals searching for a more solid religious foundation to their lives. Some believe in strict adherence to the tenets of the Bible. For example, the Christian Reconstructionists advocate following the Mosaic Law as outlined in the Old Testament Books of Leviticus and Deuteronomy. There are those, disenchanted with the mainstream of modern medicine, who are newly exploring the healing powers of faith as practiced by Christian Science, or the remedies of holistic therapies. There is a call for "a new Protestant ethic of responsibility, collective as well as individual. Cultural currents have been telling us that we as a nation can no longer condone indulging ourselves at the expense of our children and our future."[29] "Increasing numbers of baby boomers (the 77 million Americans born between 1946 and 1964) who left the fold years ago are turning religious again, but many are traveling from church to church or faith to faith, sampling creeds, shopping for a custom-made God."[30] This fluidity, this experimentation, this creeping reinvolvement of religion in work, in leisure, in politics is taking place in all industrial nations. Whether it be in housing developments in Britain's 'Bible Belt' that winds through Kent and Sussex, or the doctrines of the Japanese New Religionists, or those of the Confucian revivalists in Taiwan, religious pressures are building inside the spheric system. Inhabitants are seeking to redefine their lives.

Outside, tension is growing as well. Religious fundamentalism, more than anything, expresses dissatisfaction in the status quo and desire for change. Its two most virulent and widespread expressions are Islamic Fundamentalism, whose Middle Eastern power is rising, and Pentacostal Evangelical Protestantism whose believers comprise 50 million of Latin America's 450 million inhabitants. A recent five year study, called the Fundamentalism Project, was initiated by Professor Martin Marty of the University of Chicago Divinity School and was sponsored by the American Academy of Arts and Sciences. It involved over 200 scholars from around the world and found that among many common characteristics fundamentalist creeds, "emphasize messianic or millennial beliefs in a miraculous culmination of history, with good reigning triumphantly." Nancy T. Ammerman, a sociologist from Emory University, sees fundamentalism vying with established religions, "in criticizing the culture, in imagining a world that is different and in contesting the powers of those who claim the right to tell the culture's story."[31] The numbers of those wishing to tell this different story are rising daily.

These fundamentalists range in intensity from the violent Sinhalese Buddhists of Sri Lanka and India's radical Hindu Shiv Serra (Lord Shiva's Army), to the relatively placid Episcopalian Province of Christ the King in the United States. They do share common characteristics which include: antifeminism (calling for a return to traditional family roles), a distaste for modernity, and secularism with their attendant corruption, and an adoption of symbols to differentiate them from established beliefs. What they are all saying is that in one way or another Western civilization has not worked for them. They desire change. This may involve politics. It may involve economics. It may involve terrorism. Thus, religious fundamentalism not only creates pressures from within the industrial spheres, it also energizes millions outside the gates who pound loudly, demanding that the world be run differently and that they be admitted to the power sanctums.

Religion and its ramifications will be an increasing force in the world over the coming decades. People throughout the world are simultaneously seeking more structure and more mystery in their daily lives. As it has throughout history, religion can supply both. It also can raise tensions.

NATURAL DISASTERS AND POVERTY

There are one billion people, one-fifth of the world, living below the World Bank's definition of subsistence level poverty. In the West we periodically see images of them starving in some remote location. We are increasingly able to run across them on the street corners of our cities. Given the Malthusian outlook for population versus sustenance the world is likely to experience accelerating adversity and more frequent exposure to these images.

As more people are crowded by circumstance into climatologically or ecologically fragile areas, the problems of poverty will be multiplied. Those that are forced to live in the chronically flood-prone areas of Bangladesh, or in denuded Northeast Brazil, or adjacent to volcanoes and fault lines will find themselves increasingly at risk. Urban areas with millions packed into hastily built housing will be increasingly vulnerable not only to disease but to natural forces as well. How will the First World respond? The United States recently led a United Nations military force into Somalia in an attempt to alleviate starvation and restore order. This effort, after initial successes, played itself out in an atmosphere of growing frustration and recrimination. There will be many more Somalias. Images of pot-bellied starvelings and fly-encrusted babies will be commonplace in the Western media. Whether 'have' nations like the United States continue to respond with sympathy to each crisis, whether they work to forestall them, or whether they will allow millions to perish, will be a prime determinant of world conditions over the coming years. Natural disasters will claim even more lives. Nature's winnowing will make millions face death from poverty and disease. Warfare will swell these numbers. The consciences of 'have' nations will be tested.

Bearing this in mind what seems most likely to happen is that industrial nations will be increasingly reluctant to embrace and rectify the world's injustices. They will become inured to tragedy. Already attention is being focused on one tragedy at a time. Soon First World nations will begin to tune-out the pleas of the ravaged multitudes. They will husband both their resources and energies to deal with mounting inter-spherical needs and challenges. Faced with heightened tensions and a greater sense of impotency each of the spheres will turtle deeper into its shell, ignoring Third World turbulence. This presumes a certain cynicism and callousness produced through the numbing bombardment from suffering. It has happened before. The annals of the Middle Ages, for example, are replete with such attitudes. Should this occur the hardest hit will be in areas with minimal spherical contact, such as Africa, portions of Central Asia and patches of Southeast Asia.

The tapestry depicting the coming twenty-five to fifty years shows two to four Influence Spheres huddling behind escalating ramparts attempting to prolong their vitality as a sea of turmoil boils about them.

[1] Famine, Pestilence, War, Death - or as Barbara Tuchman put it in the forward to, *A Distant Mirror,* (Alfred A. Knopf, 1978) "The disorders cannot be traced to any one cause; they were the hoofprints of more than the four horsemen of St. John's vision, which now had become seven - plague, war, taxes, brigandage, bad government, insurrection, and schism in the Church."

[2] Paul Kennedy, *Preparing for the Twenty-First Century* (Random House, NY, 1993)

[3] Fernand Braudel , *The Mediterranean and the Mediterranean World in the Age of Philip II* (Harper Colophon Books, NY, 1972 Vol. I) pp 402-403.

[4] Ibid., (Volume II) p.734.

[5] Ibid., (Volume II) p.743.

[6] an annual income of $370, i.e. subsistence level

[7] Richard Layard, Oliver Blanchard, Rudiger Dornbusch, Paul Krugman, *East West Migrations: The Alternatives* (MIT Press, 1992)

[8] Marilyn Davis, *Mexican Voices / American Dreams* (Henry Holt and Co., 1990) p. 248.

[9] Secretariat of Intergovernmental Consultants on Asylum, Refugee, and Migration Policies for Europe, North American , and Australia

[10] It had roughly doubled from the beginning of the Eleventh to the end of the Twelfth Centuries.

[11] George Holmes, *The Later Middle Ages: 1272 to 1485* (W.W. Norton Company, London , 1962) pp 136-8.

[12] Ibid., p.138.

[13] Acquired Immune Deficiency

[14] Human Immunodeficiency Virus

[15] quoted by *Associated Press*, May 16, 1993

[16] China, North Korea, India, Russia, Kazakhstan, Israel, and Pakistan

[17] *The Economist*, February 20, 1993, p. 19

[18] Ibid., p. 20.

[19] Ibid., p. 21.

[20] Leslie H. Gelb, "Asian Arms Races," *New York Times*, March 18, 1993

[21] Michael T. Klure, "The Next Great Arms Race," *Foreign Affairs* Vol. 72, No. 3, Summer 1993, p. 137.

[22] Paul Kennedy, for one, has a different view of Japan's prospects. In *Preparing for the Twenty-First Century* he states "that because of the way their society and economy are organized the Japanese are probably the people least likely to be hurt by gross and direct damage from global over population, mass migration and environmental disasters on the one hand or from globalization of production on the other." (p.138) He does note (p.160) "the possibility of threatening external events which are difficult to forecast

in advance but...cannot be dismissed, nuclear proliferation in Asia, foreign policy adventurism...a surge in Chinese power, confrontation on the Korean peninsula or in the South China Sea...any of those would confirm Japan's strategic vulnerability."

[23] South Korea, Taiwan, Hong Kong, Singapore

[24] Malaysia, Indonesia, Thailand

[25] Michael T. Klure, "The Next Great Arms Race," *Foreign Affairs* Vol. 72, No. 3, Summer 1993, p. 145.

[26] Stephan Hawking, *A Brief History of Time* (Bantam Books, London, 1988) p. 175.

[27] Steven Weinberg, Nobel Prize winning physicist and Supercollider supporter.

[28] Bryan Appleyard, "In Science We Trust," *New York Times*, Op-Ed page, April 4, 1993.

[29] Jessica Gress-Wright, "Let's Hear It for the Protestant Ethic," *New York Times,* Op-Ed page, February 8, 1992.

[30] Richard N. Ostling, "The Church Search," *Time Magazine*, April 5, 1993, p. 45.

[31] Peter Steinfels, "Fundamentalism: Last Spasm of the 20th Century," *New York Times,* April 6, 1993.

CHAPTER 8

New Combinations and Configurations

"The basic thrust of world affairs in the late Twentieth and early Twenty-First Century will be the fundamental restructuring of the global arrangements and relationships that have evolved since the voyages of Christopher Columbus and Vasco de Gama"[1] This restructuring has already begun. While new civilizations are on the way. They have not yet arrived. However, the transition into influence spheres has commenced. Its duration depends on the determination Nietszche asserted that, "there must be chaos, that out of chaos may come forth new stars. There must be chaos that new worlds may be born." Some chaos will obviously reign and it appears to be deepening. New entities will emerge. They will cover a spectrum comprising and surrounding Influence Spheres as the world enters a new century. How many spheres there will be, how long they last, and how they translate into civilizational components will be determined by the depth and breadth of the chaos, as well as by their involvement in it. Four potential combinations and their ramifications will be described in the following pages.

GERMAN SPEAKING EUROPE

The EC's framework is showing stress fractures. It is unlikely to take effect as designed. As Eastern and Western factions are gradually pried apart by internal and external pressure a reasonable EC facsimile is likely to be formed around a German speaking core, ensconced in Central Europe.

David Roche, of the investment firm Morgan Stanley, recently described a picture that could well emerge. "Whatever shape the map of Europe ultimately takes, the invisible hand of economic self-interest will do more of the drawing in the future than the politicians...As the Maastrict vision of Europe unity dissolves, a hard currency core is forming, with Germany at its heart, surrounded by Benelux, Austria, Switzerland, Sweden and a few others. For this core to prosper in security Germany has to integrate the economies of Poland, Hungary, and the Czech lands, and Slovakia into the West European economic system."[2]

Germany itself has a population of 80 million (17 million former East Germans) a Gross Domestic Product of $1.7 trillion and armed forces of 454,000. Altogether there are approximately 100 million German speakers in Central Europe. They include most of Austria and Switzerland as well as portions of Hungary, Poland, and the Czech Republic. The currencies and economies of Germany and Switzerland are among the strongest in Europe. Hungary, Poland, and the Czech Republic are the strongest of the former Eastern European Communist states. There are many precedents for German economic and political power expanding to fill vacuums left by Russia on one side or France on the other. In fact, German unity is a more persistent historical force than that underlying the EC.

In the late Eighth Century the East Franks began pulling away from Charlemagne's Empire. After a prolonged civil war the provinces of Alemannia, Bavaria, Austrasia, and Saxony set up their own state. This occurred first by partition in 843. Then, Henry I of Saxony created a more formal union in 919. In 936 his son, Otto I, formed a larger and more solid coalition of Germans, defeated their Magyar enemies and started an eastward territorial sweep.

Both Charlemagne and then Otto claimed to be legitimate successors of Augustus and the Roman Empire. Thus, the general title of Holy Roman Empire covers the various German and later Austrian configurations that lasted until the Hapsburg ruler, Francis II, formally renounced the Imperial title in 1806. From then until World War I the old Holy Roman Empire survived under the German banners of Austria-Hungary and Prussia.

Otto's confederation was shattered in turn by another civil war (1076-1122) which gave Italian elements domination over German politics. In subsequent years the first of the great German ruling families, the Hohenstaufens[3], backed by Italian interests, created an empire that spanned Europe from Sicily to the North Sea and from Silesia to Burgundy. Fragmentation eventually set in during the

Thirteenth Century and it wasn't until 1516 when the Hapsburg Empire was created in Central Europe from former Spanish possessions[4], particularly during the reign of its Emperor Charles V (1519-1556), that German unity reappeared in earnest. This empire under various names, but always under the Catholic religion, was to last until the First World War.

Following the Reformation[5], the North splintered into a welter of 300 Protestant principalities, electorates, states, and free cities. Their disarray and distress was accentuated by the religious Thirty Years War (1618-1648). But with outside help (chiefly from the Swedes and their ruler Gustavus Adophus), German Protestants permanently denied the Catholics any control over the North. The Hohenzollern family, as Electors of Brandenberg-Prussia, gradually began a process of forging Northern unity. In the 1750s under Frederick II (the Great) of Prussia, Hohenzollern influence was enhanced. After a little over a century, in 1866, Chancellor Otto von Bismark presided over the defeat of the Austrio-Hungarian Empire at Sadowa (in Bohemia east of Prague) firmly establishing Berlin as the center of German power. In 1870 he conquered France, making Germany dominant on the continent. The combined remnants of the old Holy Roman Empire, with its Prussian and Austro-Hungarian descendants, comprise the German speaking Europe of today.

While it probably won't be sudden, the transfer of European unity and vitality from Brussels to Bonn (or Berlin) should be in place by the dawn of the next century. It will result from a German desire to dictate EC economic, foreign, and defense policies, and the subsequent resentment of nations such as France and Britain. It will result from the German pride in the mighty D-mark and reluctance to see it absorbed into monetary union. It will result from Germans bridling at being the 'milk cow' to increasingly unappreciative nations. It will result from the strengthening of German ties to Eastern Europe and the loosening of its ties to the West.

Thus far Germany has pumped 10% of its Gross Domestic Product into its own Eastern territory. It has also accounted for 70% of all foreign aid to Eastern Europe and 40% of all foreign direct investment there. Exports to Germany account for 12-16% of the combined Gross Domestic Products of Hungary, Poland, and the former Czechoslovakia.

Germany's population is aging. The average German will be 50 by the year 2000. To invigorate the labor force the first task is for Germany to integrate its own Ossis.[6] Once this is accomplished, educated, hard working Central Europeans will increasingly appeal as participants in a spreading German economic base and as an alternative to immigrant 'guest' workers. Dealings within the German bloc will grow progressively easier just as relations with Western Europeans are growing more difficult. Buffeted by threatened immigration, raw material shortages, the spectre of economic retaliation and mounting Third World chaos, Germans and their co-linguists are likely to huddle increasingly closer together.

A revival of German militarism seems unlikely, except possibly for defense. Economic development within its Influence Sphere will be aggressive, however. Thus, it appears most likely that the primary force for European unity and influence in the coming decade will be its 100 million German speakers.

FUNDAMENTAL ISLAM

Fundamental Islam, along with the Evangelical Protestantism of Latin America, is serving as the religion that speaks loudest for the world's disadvantaged. It is simple in doctrine. It is egalitarian in aspect, not in its inter-gender attitudes but in its bestowal of equal importance on each of the faithful in the eyes of Allah. It empowers believers in ways their short and desperate lives cannot. It also happens to be anti-Western and anti-establishment. This is so, precisely because the West and its allied rulers are the ones that have amassed resources and controlled events while the poor, ordinary people have grown more destitute. These conditions prevail with intermittent intensity throughout the Islamic belt that stretches from Indonesia across the bottom of Asia and the top of Africa to Morocco. Fundamentalism is a way for these anonymous poor to channel the energy of their disappointments and deprivations and feel for an instant that they are the equal of American millionaires or Saudi oil princes. It is the age-old egalitarian power of fervent religion, unifying otherwise disparate souls, welding the weak, the hungry, and the impotent into a political, economic, and possibly military strike force. This energy over time has touched many millions whether they be Christian or Hindu or Zoroastrian. It is this force that is now boiling to the surface in numerous sites throughout the Muslim world. Its ultimate goal will be the control both of the seats of religious authority, represented by Mecca and Medina and also economic power - signified by oil Whether Fundamental Islam in any form achieves these ends is one of the critical variables for the Twenty-First Century.

Francis Fukuyama sums up the situation neatly, "Islam constitutes a systematic and coherent ideology, just like liberalism and communism, with its own code of morality and doctrine of political and social justice. The appeal of Islam is potentially universal, reaching out to all men as men, and not just to members of a particular ethnic or national group. And Islam has indeed defeated liberal democracy in many parts of the Islamic world, posing a grave threat to liberal practices even in countries where it has not achieved political power directly."[7]

Islam started with the hijra[8] of the Prophet Mohammed from Mecca to Medina in the year 622. The religion began to spread rapidly following the Prophet's death in 632. By 711 soldiers and imams had spread both the holy Qur'an and the Arabic language over a swath of the globe extending from Multan in Sind to Lisbon. For an historical moment Islam controlled the largest unified territory and population of any empire on earth. But, inevitably, it sunk into torpor, factionalism, and squabbling. Vigor was regenerated after the Mongols sacked the Caliphate[9] capital of Baghdad, toppling its weakening ruler. The catalyst was Sufi[10] mysticism. This renewed vitality lasted roughly from 1300 to 1600, and eventually developed into three distinct elements which divided the Islamic world into segments that have relevance in the present day.

One element emanated from the infiltration, in the mid 1200s, of Turkic peoples from Asia into Anatolia. Under their leader, Osman, they set up a state in 1301 that eventually was to grow into the Ottoman Empire. The empire reached its first peak under Suleiman the Magnificent, its ruler from 1520 to 1566.

Another Turkic people migrated from Central Asia into India and created the Islamic Delhi Sultanate[11] in 1206 which lasted until it was superseded by Babur, the first Mughul, in 1526. The Mughuls were yet another Central Asian Islamic warrior tribe. They created an empire on the Indian sub-continent. It rose to full flowering under Babur's grandson, Akbar, who reigned from 1556 to 1605. Both the Ottoman and Mughul Empires were Sunni[12] Muslim. Sunnism still retains the majority of Islamic believers as its adherents.

The third element was a different sect, the Shi'is[13] or Shiites. They had existed as a small offshoot of the Islamic faith since the late Seventh Century, but rose to new heights when Ismail Safavi seized Tabriz and control of Persia in 1500, and proclaimed himself Shah.[14] Shah Ismail I began the Safavid Empire which reached its height under Abbas I (the Great), ruler from 1587 to 1629. Abbas' domain extended from Kandahar in the east, northward to just below Samarkand and to Tiflis and Basra in the west. The period of the late Sixteenth and early Seventeenth Centuries was the era of three great Islamic empires. This era set the stage for the ethnic segmentation, the yearning for imperial revivalism, and the inter-religious conflicts that can be currently seen throughout the Muslim world.

At present there are the Muslims of Southeast and South Central Asia with their origins in India. They extend from Indonesia and Malaysia to Pakistan. There are the Shia who are centered in Iran. They speak Farsi and reach into Central Asia (Tajiks), into the Caucasus (Azeris) and into Southern Iraq. There are the primarily Sunni Arabs, who stretch from Iraq to Morocco. Finally, there are the Turks (also Sunni) whose religious and ethnic influence follow the path of the old Ottomans from Central Asia into the Balkans.

The bastions of Sunni religious and political establishment are generally governed by Western-oriented elites and include Wahabi Saudi Arabia, NATO member Turkey, the Egypt of Hosni Mubarak, the Morocco of King Hassan, Suharto's Indonesia and Pakistan. Sunni renegades, such as the leaders of Syria, Iraq, and Libya, have ruthlessly repressed dissension and played political forces off against each other to retain power. Shiite Iran has unabashedly followed a defiant, deeply religious, aggressively anti-Western course, blazing the pathway for fundamentalism's revival.

Many of the world's over one billion Muslims exist outside states where their religion comprises the majority. Several examples are the 1 million Muslims (largely from India and Pakistan) in Britain, the 3 million Muslims (largely from North Africa) in France, and the 1.7 million 'guest' workers (mostly Turks) in Germany. China has 15 million Muslims who make up 50 percent (even after importation of Han Chinese colonists) of the strategically important Western border province of Xinjiang. In the United States there will be more Muslim-Americans than Jewish-Americans by the year 2000. In Bosnia Muslims are at the center of a bloody reincarnation of ancient hatreds.

It is extremely important to realize that all Muslim 'fundamentalists' are not Shiites linked to Iran. They are not all committed to an anti-Western religious state or a revival of Islamic glory. What they seek is a better life, and fundamentalism is viewed as the best means for its attainment. Thus, Islamic fundamentalism prospers where conditions are the worst. It is true that anti-Westernism is a prime component. It flourishes as a straw man erected by leaders so that the disadvantaged can have a ready target upon which to focus their general dissatisfaction and envy. Policy makers in the West often over-react to the rhetoric of tirades and demonstrations. Their own actions often galvanize multitudes behind radical factions whose tenets they normally might not support. A good example of this situation can be found in Algeria.

Modern Islamic fundamentalism probably began with the creation of the Muslim Brotherhood in Egypt in the 1920s. Its initial, as well as its current members, were mostly Sunni. In fact, most of the militants who today call for strict enforcement of the sharya (Islamic law) and repudiation of Western corruption are Sunni. This is true even for those with strong connections to Iran, such as the National Economic Front in the Sudan, the Islamic Salvation Front in Algeria, or the fundamentalists among the Farsi speaking Tajiks[15]. Even in pro-Western countries like Saudi Arabia and Pakistan conservative religious elements, which heretofore have echoed the policies of established government, have begun to distance themselves calling for a more militant stance. In areas where loyalties are divided, such as Afghanistan and Central Asia, Sunni and Shia fundamentalists sometimes coexist, sometimes collide. Westerners need to realize that "Iran's main influence comes from the power of example."[16] Just as opposition to the state of Israel has provided a lightning rod for militant fundamentalists, Iran's implacable defiance of the affluent West has served as a beacon. As long as the overwhelming majority of Muslims remain enveloped in poverty leaders who propose rigorous opposition to the 'haves' will gain a following. Thus, fundamentalism has often spanned the chasm of religious and ethnic division, creating political, if not philosophic, ties based more upon common deprivation than upon a concomitance of belief.

The terrorists who reputedly hijacked aircraft or blew up New York's World Trade Center in 1993, or the Jamaat-al-Musilmen of Trinidad who created a bloody uprising in 1990, or the various groups threatening tranquillity across the globe are given their importance by the fact that virtually all of the world's 1 billion Muslims live in poverty and squalor, without reasonable hope of extrication. They are also given importance by the fact that Muslim nations sit upon one of the world's most vital resources - oil. This raises critical questions for the next century.

Will Muslim ruling elites and industrial world nations continue to receive virtually all of the benefits from the pumping of oil? Will Europe and the United States continue to treat the important democratic, capitalistic stronghold of Turkey[17] as an outsider which occasionally receives scraps from the Western table, but is not included at the real council sessions?[18] Will the West continue to regard disadvantaged Muslims aggressively pleading for recognition and for alleviation of poverty as dangerous 'fundamentalist' fanatics, while approving those co-religionists who pander to Western interests and pocketbooks? To what extent will industrial nations continue to be willing to spend billions to prop up threatened establishment Islamic regimes such as Saudi Arabia, Kuwait, and Egypt and to actively defend Gulf oil fields from military threat?

Continuation of a policy of financial dichotomy towards Muslims, and ignoring the distress signals of the Islamic disadvantaged, could prove to be calamitous to oil hungry Europe and Japan. As was seen in the Sixteenth and Seventeenth Centuries, Islamic potency does not necessarily depend upon its unity. The Industrial World can no longer rely on the fact that there are many theological and ideological differences in the Muslim world as insurance against its rise as a global force. The luck of nature, or the gift of Allah, which has placed oil under Islamic states as far flung as Indonesia, Kazakhstan, Kuwait, and Algeria has given them the potential to control the economic future of the many industrial nations. Among these nations only the United States and its hemispheric neighbors have any immediate prospect of creating energy self-sufficiency. There is no doubt that the Islamic militancy, that is simmering under the surface virtually everywhere, will have as a prime objective wresting control over oil from the hegemony of the First World. Whether this effort will be successful, whether there will be one or two Islamic Influence Spheres, and whether the latent hostility of the Muslim billion is transformed into a real factor in the world power equation depends largely on the mental attitude of those now destitute. Current readings of their state of mind do not provide optimistic omens for Western prospects.

LATIN CODA TO THE AMERICAN MOVEMENT

There are 450 million people in Latin America. It is the most urbanized area of a mostly urban world.[19] Why would it be the type of asset that will attract closer ties with North America? The tripartite answer is - resources, markets, and labor.

Of the 450 million Latin Americans, Brazil contains about 150 million, Mexico 88 million, Argentina 32 million and Columbia 30 million. This compares to 250 million in the United States and 26 million in Canada. While the populations of both the United States and Canada are growing older as the new century commences, Latin America will have increasing numbers of people in those most productive and highest consuming age groups, the 20s and 30s.

The United States has a Gross Domestic Product of about $6 trillion, Canada's Gross Domestic Product is about $500 billion. Latin America's Gross Domestic Product, in aggregate, is slightly over $1.2 trillion. Brazil at $400 billion, Mexico at $300 billion, and Argentina at $125 billion account for the lion's share. Argentina, Chile, Mexico and Venezuela all will average real Gross Domestic Product growth of over 3.5% in both 1992 and 1993, outgrowing their wealthier North American neighbors.

The United States has a Gross Domestic Product per head of $20,000 and industrial output per head of $5,000. Canada's figures are $19,000 and $6,500. Brazil and Mexico's output are each around $2,600 and $800 per head. Latin America, as a whole, has per capita Gross Domestic Product of $2,300. and per capita industrial output of $715. The Latin markets are growing rapidly but still have plenty of expansion room. A measure of the distance to be traveled can be seen in the fact that despite recent improvements, Gross Domestic Product per head in Latin America is still in real terms roughly where it was in the 1970s. At that time this level was twice that of South Korea and Taiwan. Now it is half of their output.

Maybe the most important economic factor of all is energy. The United States imports over 50% of its oil requirements and is less than 75% energy self-sufficient. Canada Mexico, and Venezuela are huge net energy exporters. The North and South American economies thus have the combined potential to be energy self-sufficient in the future, the only Influence Sphere to be so positioned.

The Latin American nations of Brazil, Chile, Peru, Guyana, Surinam, Jamaica, and Bolivia are all rich in non-energy mineral resources. Many of these have been only partially developed. They provide an excellent base for industrial development. United States companies have grasped this and their direct investment in Latin America leapt from a level of $30 billion in 1987 to $50 billion in 1992. Latin imports of United States goods rose 16% to $5.8 billion in 1991 and went up a further 18% to $67 billion in 1992, cementing a favorable balance of trade for the North.

Latin America is not only energy self-sufficient and resource rich, it also can provide all of its own food, and has empty territory to absorb population growth.

In the decade of the 1980s Latin American nations took many steps which will make themselves more desirable political and economic partners. Democratic reforms proliferated, removing generals from their seats of governmental power. Runaway inflation was reversed, in most cases dramatically. Debt and deficit levels were reduced. Privatization spread. Outflows of private capital turned into inflows. Equity markets rose, and broadened.

The story is not all positive. Income distribution is more skewed in these nations than in most of the world's regions. For example, the top 20% of Latin Americans earners are 21 times richer than the bottom 20%, whereas in Asia the difference is only 9 times. Democracy is still delicate in most countries, with a fall back into authoritarianism possible at any time. The same fragility could be ascribed to inflation and debt levels, neither of which have been reduced below the danger level. Combined Latin American debt service still equals 30% of its exports. There are rebels roaming the hinterlands in many nations. Both drug production and distribution are major economic and social factors in Columbia, Peru, and Bolivia. In addition, there are severe environmental challenges, such as the depletion of the Brazilian rain forest. Finally, the problem of satisfactory urban living will obviously need to be faced with cities such as Sao Paulo, Brazil (population 15 million) and Mexico City (20 million) mushrooming, seemingly uncontrollably.

Even after all the cautions have been raised, Latin America still emerges as a positive contributor in combination with its Northern neighbors. Most of its new, young, democratically elected leaders were educated in the United States. Its fastest growing religion is Evangelical Protestantism, a United States import. The United States itself has 25 million citizens of Hispanic heritage and they are growing faster than the population as a whole. Finally, Latin America has taken the first steps toward regional cooperation. Brazil, Argentina, Uruguay, and Paraguay have signed a formal economic pact - Mercosur. Mexico is in the process of formulating agreements with Chile and also with Venezuela and Columbia. The Central American Common market may well be revived. There is also NAFTA, welding Mexico to its northern neighbors. Whatever its form, greater regional cooperation is inevitable over the coming decade, and it will grow progressively stronger in the coming century.

Presuming the nations of North and South America can keep their internal houses in order, they possess some significant advantages over other areas. Their borders will be free from the possibility of encroachment by large scale military conflict. The pressures of migration will be less than in other areas. Their region is self-sufficient in most key resources, particularly energy and food. A long history of trade and cooperation between the various entities will facilitate the formation of additional patterns. There is enough territorial room to absorb projected population growth. A Latin America-North America combination could easily be the most economically and socially vibrant of the several Influence Spheres. Its vitality could extend well into the next century.

CHINA ASTRIDE THE FLAMES OF EAST ASIA

East Asia may well manifest the world's most difficult and traumatic theater as the new century opens. By the first quarter of the next century China and India combined will have 3 billion people. Imagine the resources, and the space, needed to support and house 3 billion people! Eastern Asia is not well endowed with either mineral resources or agricultural productive capability, particularly in relationship to its population. The contest between China and India for control of the wherewithal to feed, clothe, and shelter their billions will be the most important of the many conflicts to be played out on this stage.

Japan is just past its peak of economic and political influence which occurred in the late 1980s. Buffeted by economic recession, financial instability, and political scandal, Japan is feeling the first repercussions of its highly leveraged, strictly regimented governing blend of the old boy network with corporate committeeism. One required adjustment will be the need to undergo some financial restructuring to reliquify its banks, insurance companies, and manufacturers. Another will be the social engineering needed in response both to the demands of Japanese women, for enhanced participation in many sectors, and to the problems of a rapidly aging work force. Leadership, both corporate and governmental, is currently staffed by bureaucracies; men selected from a narrow range of universities and backgrounds. This will need to be expanded. In addition, Japan will have to escalate its military spending in an attempt to protect its far flung network of suppliers, production sites, and customers. In a part of the world which remembers the Japanese Empire with very little fondness this won't be easy. Japan's search for allies will be extensive. The most logical candidate is Russia (or its Eastern components) with its abundant resources, large army, and strategic position on China's northern borders. As Walter McDougall described in his book, "Let the Sea Make A Noise",[20] the interplay between Japan, Russia, China, and the United States in the North Pacific and its littoral has been one of the most important determinants of historical trends.

Almost everyone acknowledges that China has enormous potential for the future. The odds are favorable that it will eventually emerge to dominate East Asia economically, politically, and militarily. But that may not happen until a long and bloody struggle is completed. With two dangerous potential foes along its Northern and Southern flanks (Russia and India), China's relations with its other militarily and economically powerful neighbors will be delicate.

Pakistan, long a China supporter, can provide some help to counterbalance India. Muslim neighbors to the West, if they are friendly, can offer some insulation for Tibet and the empty, but strategic, Western provinces of Qinhai, Gansu, and Xinjiang. In Southeast Asia the attitudes of Vietnam with its huge army; of Thailand with its economic muscle; of Malaysia and Indonesia with their resources; of Cambodia with its warring factions and United Nations occupation, all will be important variables. In the Northeast, the Koreas, together or separately, will provide an important fulcrum between the resources and territory of the continent and the power of their traditional enemy Japan. China will need to develop an ability to juggle all of these elements amid rising demographic desperation and increasing arms accumulation. History is replete with examples both of Chinese successes and failures under similar conditions.

Militarily, China's ability to keep from fighting strong foes on two fronts will determine its survival as a single entity. Economically, its ability to wean the resources of Indonesia and the productive might of South Korea, Taiwan, Singapore, and Thailand from their Japanese and Western orientation will prove a difficult but necessary task. Politically, China will have to resist its own historical tendency to divide under pressure. The productive South, including Hong Kong, has always sought independence. The Southern economy and entrepot are vital to China's future and must be harnessed and retained for the nation to accumulate any form of world power status, not to mention East Asian hegemony. China's Muslim West, also with a tendency toward independence, is vulnerable to incursions and influence from Islamic Central Asia as well as from Russia. The permutations and combinations of these various factors will keep China and its environs in a state of turbulence. In addition, Chinese planners will have to ask, if the multitudes come boiling out of the Indian sub continent seeking food and room, where will they be stopped? Will it be at the Himalayas? Will it be in Myanmar? Will an Indian empire once again extend from Indonesia to Tibet and Afghanistan? The answers to these questions will define the nature of the China-India concussion as well as its reverberations.

This discussion has been conducted thus far as if warfare in East Asia is a virtual certainty. It is not. There are choices. They involve explosive demographic and political issues. While conflict is not inevitable it is highly likely, unless these issues are successfully defused and the regional arms race is reversed. Before China can emerge victorious and dominant it will most probably endure invasion, secession, and privation. War and its accompanying starvation are apt to drastically reduce populations in Eastern Asia. They will also affect economic output. China's day of regional triumph and regional omnipotency will likely come, but it may not arrive until the century's latter half. By that time the rest of the world's reaction to the Asian inferno will have determined civilization's course and the Influence Spheres will have undergone transformation.

THE ROLE OF INTERNATIONAL ORGANIZATIONS

In the post-World War II period the United Nations has served as the world's primary international organization. It has come together on occasion militarily to serve as an agent of the United States foreign policy : Korea in 1950; The Gulf War in 1991; Somalia in 1992. It has also served, with uneven effectiveness, as a peacekeeping agent in a wide array of situations from the Middle East to Southeast Asia. It has functioned as a forum for international discussions and disputes to be aired. Perhaps its most enduring work has been done through special purpose organizations like the World Health Organization, UNICEF[21] and the International Monetary Fund.

Some analysts[22] have projected a future in which the United Nations strengthens, becoming an even more important factor in halting aggression and depredations, in resolving crises and in fomenting interaction. While this scenario is possible, it is not probable. The main restraints are financial and political.

The world is strapped for cash. Only 18 of the United Nations' 180 members met their dues payment deadline on January 31, 1993. The United States (which pays 25% of the regular budget through dues, and 30% of the peacekeeping budget) was $846 million in arrears at the end of 1992. The cost of peacekeeping has risen dramatically. In 1986-7 it was $364 million, in 1991-2 it was $1.4 billion, in 1992-3 it was $3.6 billion. The United Nations had 55,000 peacekeepers around the world at the end of 1991-1992 fiscal year. The figure doubled the following year, with calls for more troops coming in regularly. Although the average United Nations member spends only $1.40 on peacekeeping, for every $1,000 spent on its own defense, there is an increasing reluctance by members to contribute this money and turn over military assets and policy to United Nations command.

The reason is political. In Article 43 of the United Nations Charter there is authorization for a standing military force. There is a movement underway by some delegates to enforce this article for the first time. The May 1993 takeover of a United Nations Somalia command, including United States forces, by a Turkish general was heralded as a first step in that direction. Whether the industrial nations will be willing to cede their sovereignty to an organization increasingly responsive to Third World voting power is problematical. Whether a United Nations quick response peacekeeping force paid for by a specially created fund could effectively deal with the multitude of expected conflicts is another question. Whether the United Nations can overcome its bureaucratic and political constraints, and decide where and how to involve itself, poses still another riddle. The sustained reluctance of European nations to support attempts in Bosnia to stem Serb aggression is a manifestation of the difficulties in making decisions and reacting quickly. So is the hostility of the United Nations' Islamic numbers to Western-proposed 'solutions' that do not adequately protect Bosnian Muslims. Thus, it seems unlikely that any standing force for either peacemaking or peacekeeping will be accepted or authorized by the industrial nations.

As the monetary power of the various sphere leaders offsets each other, and as the voting power of the Third World builds, the purpose of the United Nations will be tested. Will it evolve into a true international body serving the interest of members in a democratic manner? Will it falter as the elite industrial nations, now dominating the Security Council, find themselves unable to exercise their national will through the United Nations? Except for brief flashes of support the United States has been consistently critical and unwilling to cede sovereignty in any form. In the 1980s the Reagan Administration so strongly disapproved of United Nations policies that it stopped paying its bills. For most of its life the United Nations has stood far back from the world's center stage, castigated as misguided, mismanaged and ineffectual by Western leaders, including Presidents of the United States. After a brief spell in the spotlight, when it enforced the policies of the United States in a one superpower world, it seems once again destined for the periphery.

There are other international organizations. Virtually all of them exist for specific purposes. Interpol[23], which was founded in 1938 with 25 members and now contains 125 is one of the better known. NATO, although the most enduring of the military alliances, is experiencing difficulty in defining structure and purpose. OPEC was founded in 1960 and seems to have survived wars, political differences and ethnic disparity. The International Red Cross (or Red Crescent in Muslim nations), which was founded in 1882, Amnesty International, and the World Wildlife Fund are three of these special-purpose, often humanitarian groupings. Such organizations should continue to function, as they often provide unique and necessary services. International organizations, in general, reached their post-World War II height of status in the early 1990s, highlighted by the Gulf War military action of the United Nations, and are likely to experience a waning influence.

THE SPHERIC WORLD

Many aspects of this postulated realm of spherism are grim. Much of the world will be engulfed by great suffering over the next twenty of thirty years. In many ways this will be a corrective process for past excesses. It will also be compensation for the uneven and incomplete nature of technology's advances. Barbara Tuchman noted sagely that, "in real life every age is a checkerboard of light and dark."[24] One dramatic example was Fourteenth Century Europe. At that time there lived, amid the Black Death, The Little Ice Age, and the Hundred Years War, Chaucer, Petrach, Dante, and Giotto, all sparkling individuals with dazzling achievements. We should remember that unsettled period which gave birth to great universities in Rome, Pisa, Grenoble, Cologne, and Heidelberg as well as to several colleges at Oxford. In those depths of the Dark Ages John Wyclif, Giovanni Boccaccio and Jan Hus helped sow the seeds of the Renaissance and Reformation. Technological advancement, great luxury and magnificent creativity existed alongside destitution and destruction. Similarly, in the coming decades millions will live fulfilling lives. Creativity will flourish in countless ateliers. Individuals of greatness will flash across the screen of existence. But in every sense the world will be in a period of transition. Possibly it will be characterized as a 'Dark Age'. The next civilizations are not yet before us. The search for their ingredients will allow us to measure the degree to which our societies will be compatible rather than confrontational.

Braudel was not optimistic. "The present crisis which refuses to go away is more sinister, as if it cannot manage to show its true face, or find a label or model which would explain it and reassure us. It is not so much a hurricane as a flood, with the water rising slowly but alarmingly, under a sky obstinately gray and waterlogged. All the foundations of economic life and all the lessons of experience past and present seem to be being challenged."[25] Evolution will occur as it always has. Those of us in the First World who possess the advantages can significantly influence its nature.

It is up to us to rise to the challenges. We cannot stem the flood of new civilization. However, we can change our ways to help moderate it. We can alter our standard of living so as to preserve the environment and have the wherewithal to redistribute some income. We can rearrange our value system to provide a more solid civilizational foundation. We can reduce the damaging impact of too much technology. We can suspend arms sales and destroy weapons. These measures may not be enough. There may still be the prospect of too many people with too few resources and space. The necessary adjustments may be too dramatic and too pervasive to be made willingly by any society. Our primary option is not to eliminate adjustments, it is to determine whether they are made involuntarily, or as part of a designed scheme which buffers the reverberations.

It is this voluntary/involuntary aspect of adjustments that human nature never seems able to anticipate and overcome. The fact that most change ends up being involuntary causes acute pain. The biggest task facing the period of spherism is to produce a level of moderation during the civilizational transition which minimizes chaos and puts a damper on suffering.

---

[1] Leftan Stavrianos, *The Promise of the Coming Dark Age* (W.H. Freeman & Co., NY, 1976) p. 167.

[2] David C. Roche, "Europe's Ill Winds: Good For Eastern Europe" *Morgan Stanley Incorporated Newletter*, November 17, 1992.

[3] The others were Hohenzollerns of Prussia, the Hapsburgs of Austria, and the Wittlesbachs of Bavaria.

[4] The Hapsburgs had assumed control of the Spanish Empire in 1438.

[5] Martin Luther posted his 95 theses on the church door of Wittenberg in 1517, starting the Reformation.

[6] former inhabitants of East Germany

[7] Francis Fukuyama, T*he End of History and the Last Man* (The Free Press, NY 1992) p. 45.

[8] Albert Hourani, *A History of the Arab Peoples* (The Belknap Press of Harvard University Press, Cambridge, MA 1991) p. 17. hijra or hegira - "Seeking protection by settling in a place other than ones own. In later Islamic centuries it would be used to mean the abandonment of a pagan or wicked community for one living in accordance with the moral teaching of Islam"

[9] Caliphs from the word khalifa - successor to the Prophet.

[10] *A Short History of the Arab Peoples* p. 72. An Anglicanized form of tasawwhf - the Arabic equivalent of the word mysticism, "a believer meditating on its (the Qur'an) meaning might be filled with a sense of the overwhelming transcendence of God and the total dependence of all creatures on him."

[11] Sultan - holder of power.

[12] *A History of the Arab Peoples* pp 36-7. The Prophet's habitual behavior in Arabic is called sunna. The belief in the importance of the Qur'an and the practice of sunna is known as Sunnism, or practice of the first principles.

13 *A Short History of the Arab Peoples* pp 181-186 The Shi'is believe that the Prophet's true line is 'Ali ibn Abi Talib, an early convert to Islam. He was a cousin of Mohammud who married the Prophet's daughter Fatima. He lost a struggle for power and for the control of the Caliphate and was assassinated in 661. His followers became the partisans of 'Ali, the shi 'at Ali, or Shi'is.

14 Shah - king of kings.

15 Of the Central Asian Republics' 60 million Muslims there are about 10 million Farsi speaking (the language of Iran) Tajiks. However, most Tajiks are Sunni.

16 "Islam Resumes Its March," *The Economist*, April 4, 1992

17 Turkey is the Muslim world's only secular democracy.

18 Turkey is a member of NATO and was heavily relied upon in the Gulf War, but is not being welcomed into the EC.

19 Latin America was 70% urban in 1990, by 2010 it will be 75% urban.

20 Walter A. McDougall, *Let the Sea Make A Noise...A History of the North Pacific from Magellan to MacArthur* (Basic Books, 1994)

21 United Nations Children's Education Fund

22 Including the 11 person blue-ribbon panel set up in 1993 by the Ford Foundation and chaired by Paul Volker.

23 International Criminal Police Organization

24 Barbara Tuchman, *A Distant Mirror* (Alfred A. Knopf, NY, 1978) p. 448.

25 Fernand Braudel, "The Perspective of the World," *Civilization & Capitalism 15th-18th Century, Volume 3* (Harper and Row Publishers, NY, 1984) p. 81.

PART III

Inside the Third World Order

"Things filled men with fear: the more things they had, the more they had to fear. Things had a way of riveting themselves onto the soul and then telling the soul what to do."

Bruce Chatwin
The Songlines
Penguin Books, London, 1988

CHAPTER 9

Quadruple Basics

As the modern world heads towards a new century the nations comprising its main industrial, financial, and philosophical forces are increasingly beginning to question and grow defensive about many of their principles and structures. Paul Johnson alluded to this societal self-doubt in his most recent book. "Certainly, by the last decade of the century, some lessons had plainly been learned. But it was not clear whether the underlying evils which had made possible its catastrophic failures and tragedies - the rise of moral relativism, the decline of personal responsibility, the repudiation of Judeo-Christian values, not the least the arrogant belief that men and women could solve all the mysteries of the universe by their own unaided intellects - were in the process of being eradicated. On that would depend the chances of the Twenty-First century becoming, by contrast, an age of hope for mankind."[1]

The industrial/technological nations are scrambling to find answers to their most pressing problems. There are no easy formulae to rectify these complex situations. It is ironic that the simplest and most direct path to solution may be deceptively near at hand, a part of these nations since their beginnings. Whether the First World follows this route of introspection or not is open to question. What is far less questionable is that, should it be taken, this route will prove a road of discovery leading straight to the civilizations of the Twenty-First Century.

Ensconced in the world community today are a number of societies that have survived more or less intact for over a thousand years. A brief look at the composition and operation of four selected representatives may provide some clues as to how an 'age of hope' might be achieved. These representatives are relatively distinct. In other places the picture may be slightly blurred. In all areas these are lessons to be learned, even by the most hidebound and arrogant technological world denizens. Nowhere is this more illustrative than in the United States, where "after years of urging Native Americans to take up our ways, however, we may have at last realized that it is time to take up theirs."[2] It is among such native communities that the path towards solutions commences. We have traced the courses of First and Second World crises. It behooves us now to take up the trail of Third World promise.

Two of the four selected societies are hunter-gatherer in origin and tradition: the Bushmen of the Kalahari Desert and the Aboriginal tribes of Australia. The other two are sedentary farmers and artisans: the Maya of Guatemala and Mexico, and the Balinese. Their combined attributes and characteristics are replicated in many crannies of the globe in many settings. Before inspecting these societies it is vital to remember one basic assumption. None of them can be appropriately called 'primitive' or 'unsophisticated'. Their people have demonstrated high intelligence levels in many areas over many centuries. They have qualities and methodologies that may prove useful to those of us in the First World embarking tremulously upon the Twenty-First Century. If we will but look and listen we can benefit from both study and osmosis. The difficult part will be developing the habit of opening our eyes and especially our minds. We may not be able to transplant ancient societies into our industrial corpus, but we can increase its opportunity for survival by judicious transfusion.

The Bushmen are a remarkable and an ancient people. They have developed intricate methods for sustaining themselves in harsh and delicate surroundings. At first glance the typical industrial/technological resident wouldn't believe the Kalahari capable of supporting settlement much less allowing it to flourish for millennia. A European who resided among them for many years captured the situation. "We have much to learn from the Bushmen...for the Bushman has evolved a solution to life that for all the indications to the contrary, isn't pure survival...He has got nearer than we superior beings might ever do to the art of living in keeping with his environment."[3] Many thousands of years ago these people[4] made their way down the continent of Africa from the cradle of human evolution on the shores of Lake Victoria. Until quite recently (less than a thousand years ago) they were the sole inhabitants of Southern Africa. The Bushmen/San are small and wiry in build, fawn in color and speak a Khosian family language comprised of a series of glottal clicks. Their society, 'conceivably represents the longest continuous evolutionary tenancy of any one region on earth.'[5]

Bushmen have always followed their nomadic routes in small, extended family bands whose composition fits the ecological tolerance of the land covered. Sharing and foraging, their existence is based upon a deep knowledge of local flora[6] and fauna which has allowed them to persevere. As closely knit as they may be, "they know that when times are bad the group can only live together by breaking up. To save the fabric of their small society they must sometimes take it apart."[7] Flexibility, then, geared to the tenor of climate and ecology has facilitated adjustment and prolonged survival. These people recognized at an early stage that rigidity meant extinction.

Bushmen also have a complex system of territorial rights employing landmarks and water holes. They have a sense of individual or family property, as well, which involves those elements of primary societal importance such as water, ostrich eggs, and honey. Nevertheless, sharing is critical to their collective survival, as is an ability to recognize geography. Both of these traits are expressed or imparted through the extended family. For example, infants learn to speak and to identify by repetition while being carried on an almost continual journey[8] - always by their mother's brother. It is through many interactions such as this that familial bonds are formed, cooperation is ensured, and a system of government is developed. "Both authority and responsibility are shared by the elders of the band and the extent of one's influence depends as much on one's intelligence, initiative and example as on one's guile."[9]

An expertise at mimicry, which utilizes animal postures and disguises, forms the basis for hunting, entertainment, and warfare. The result of these attributes is that Bushmen have an ability to blend with their surroundings which has continuously caused both opponents and observers to marvel. Their sense of direction and location achieved through a mental mapping and recognition system is also remarkable. These people commit to memory hundreds of square miles of regularly traversed terrain. They also have an almost photographic retention of patterns of flora and geography of areas being seen for the first time. Bushmen seem to innately realize the limits of the land they inhabit and react to them. In addition to these attributes they possess a varied culture. Their art, depicting aspects of daily life, has been preserved in cave paintings predating recorded history. They are a deeply religious people. Bushmen worship a Supreme Being, 'Guthe', and fear its evil alter-ego, 'Thoa'. A similar dichotomy is attached to virtually every aspect of their lives. Their beliefs require respect and concern for the plants and animals upon which they rely, and these are treated as living beings. For example, like many native peoples, the Bushmen beg forgiveness from those animals it is necessary to kill and those plants it is necessary to harvest.

The Bushman, "lives a socialized role by allowing each of his fellow men the opportunity to live his life as long as he doesn't interfere with the peace and tranquillity of the society to which he belongs."[10] This sounds simple, but as we all know it is anything but a simple principle to follow. The more they are studied the more one realizes that Bushmen have an innate understanding of how their society should work and of how individuals should relate. It is also evident that they are careful to keep to every element in their world in its proper perspective. There is, "an unbroken communion between these small, yellowish aboriginal people and their descendants and the wild, beautiful, natural world surrounding them."[11] Family community, beliefs, ancestors and ecology are all woven together to form a social fabric that is alive and has endured.

It is obvious that apart from the aftermath of some disaster, a hunter-gatherer society is not a realistic option for most people today. What can be an option is to understand ways in which we might emulate an existence that produces balance among its various facets and components. We may develop ways by which these examples can be tested, learned, and absorbed. The options now facing industrial/technological nations bear resemblance to those impacting the Bushmen when the ecology of their segment of the Kalahari changes. Are we as well programmed as they for adjustment? Understanding how they adjust, why they adjust, and when they adjust is much more than inspecting primitive tribalism. It could be the key to our survival as a civilized entity.

"Why then are so many Western pokesmen in the depths of despair. Why do they foresee gloom and doom, or urge the acceptance of a technocratic elite as the only way out of our mounting difficulties?"[12] Maybe it is because we: in the First World, the Industrial World, the Technological World, haven't learned the lesson the Maya learned the hard way. It is to the eternal credit of the Maya, as a people, that they have sustained a vibrant societal presence even after their civilization, one of the greatest the world has ever known, collapsed, mainly from over-reliance on technology. They did this by reverting to their basic principles, those that had carried their people to prominence before technology ran amok.

The people who became the mighty Maya began to settle in the lowlands of the present Guatemala, Belize, and Mexico (now called the Petén) around 2000 B.C.[13] Over the years they created a civilization which flourished and they exercised regional domination, especially during the Classic Maya period which lasted from 200 A.D. to 900 A.D. Mayan civilization then staggered, evaporating in the lowlands and moving north to the Yucatan peninsula in a somewhat diluted form for another 300 to 400 years of puissance. While the cause of the Petén Maya civilization's demise is not precisely known, most research indicates that it had a lot to do with the same sort of problems the world's developed nations face today.

The Maya were a mystical people believing in spirit life, dream interpretation, and time travel. They also were highly structured, determinedly scientific and technologically sophisticated. They invented the concept of the number zero,[14] probably before the Arabs. They were skilled astronomers and mathematicians who could plot the orbit of their sacred planet Venus with an error factor of only sixteen seconds per year. They had a mathematical system, based on the number twenty which could handle extremely complex calculations. Their calendar extended forwards and backwards in a series of regular but intricate cycles designed both to record and predict. Their system of hieroglyphic writing was both syllabic and ideographic, allowing them to compose extensive books covering a variety of subjects. They farmed using raised-bed agriculture and canals, transported water by use of aqueducts and built giant causeways to connect their cities.[15]

The Maya were an urban society which governed through a sequence of city-states, much like the ancient Greeks. They built dozens of metropoli, some of which had over one-hundred thousand inhabitants and were among the largest cities in the world at the time. Great pyramidic temples as tall as twenty story buildings, rose from plazas amid multi-colored, multi-storied dwellings which resembled an Art Deco fantasy. Strolling through an ancient Maya city would have been an eye catching experience. Not only were the buildings tall and colorful, but the people, especially the elite, were dressed in brilliant, often elaborate costumes of textiles, wicker and feathers adorned with jade, obsidian, and precious metals. Artistic and architectural accomplishments were everywhere. Maya civilization was learned, ordered, and wealthy. It expanded steadily, punctuating the fragile rain forest ecology with an increasing number of cities and their attendant support systems.

Suddenly things started to go awry. While Maya cities had periodically seen their hegemony rise and fall in dynastic rhythms, around the year 800 these population centers began to cease functioning as organized, even inhabited, entities. The cause most probably originated with an overtaxing of the relatively fragile agricultural and water resources of the Petén rain forest. This was likely combined with subtle, but critical, changes in climate.[16] Warfare, which had previously been intermittent and political, became increasingly necessary to obtain the wherewithal for survival. Thus, conflict occurred more frequently and more destructively. The lowland Maya civilization, in place and powerful for a thousand years began to atrophy, scatter, and migrate. For all practical purposes the great civilization was over by the year 900.[17] But the story didn't end. The Maya culture moved North, combined with people such as the Toltec and perpetuated its basic beliefs and discoveries. It survived decimation by disease, conquest by local and external forces, and the imposition of an alien religion. It is very much alive today. Large numbers of Maya inhabit Guatemala, Mexico and parts of Belize. How did they manage to stay intact as a society through the repeated traumas of conquest, which have included more than one attempt at genocide?

An answer is contained in basic spiritual strengths which commence with a creation myth. Not unlike many other belief systems, Mayan myth depicts a people led by god-like ancestors who defeated the forces of evil in the underworld and emerged onto the sacred land as its guardians. This mythical origin and its employment in the subsequent Maya calculations based upon its determination on August 13, 3114 BC coincides with anthropological estimates of the actual initial southward migrations of the people who became the Maya. This myth encouraged an existence overlain with the uncertainty of dualities (good/evil, male/female) strongly connected with the past. It fostered a society that blended mysticism with practicality and mythology with actuality. The strength of the Mayan spiritual roots and their everyday relevance enabled their people to absorb the impositions of their conquerors while retaining their own integrity. The Maya were even able to accept the veneer of Catholicism, when the Spaniards arrived in a burst of flame and blood, while barely disturbing the heartbeat of their established beliefs.

Throughout the centuries of conquest and subjugation the underlying Maya social structure and spiritual tenets remained more or less intact. Rigoberta Menchú described this transformation. "By accepting the Catholic religion, we didn't accept a condition or abandon our culture. It was more like another way of expressing ourselves."[18] The long count[19] and other elements of the Maya calendar are still observed. Priests still assist their people to worship the traditional spirits. As in ancient times, "the prayers and ceremonies are for the whole community. We pray to our ancestors, reciting their prayers which have been known to us for a long time."[20]

There are two words in this statement which are keys to any civilizations survival - 'ancestors' and 'community'. The Maya have utilized both. Rigoberta Menchú describes the methods. "We Indians never do anything which goes against the laws of our ancestors."[21] Continuity and respect are maintained in all activities, and through them strength. Strength also emanates from another source, obligation. "My father said; 'you have a lot of responsibility; you have many duties to fulfill in our community as an adult, From now on you must contribute to the common good'."[22] Along with precedent and rights come responsibilities. Each community member has them. This has created a solid communal foundation, a foundation that has endured. Maya culture has endured with it; by valuing its past, each individual, and the earth itself. This represents a dramatic change from the rich and reckless Classic Maya period. It could be the overriding reason why, "the adoption of the Maya practices may be our only chance of saving a planet we failed to love and cherish as they did. We, like them, should consider ourselves not the owners of the earth, but its guardians."[23] Their magnificent civilization fell because Maya themselves temporarily forgot the precepts that had made them great. Their culture has endured because they managed to recapture the principle. The story of their ascension, collapse, and subsequent persistence are lessons that may be the most valuable Mayan legacy.

Bali is interesting because it was well settled and prosperous back as far as its history is recorded. It retained prosperity despite dramatic changes and frequent turmoil. The important knowledge for us to garner is how this continuity was maintained.

The island of Bali was intensely populated by an agricultural, animistic Malayo-Polynesian people as early as 300 B.C.[24] Around the year 500 A.D. the island began to be visited by Hindu traders, probably emanating through Java from the Bengali-influenced colonial empires of the Kambuja in Southern Cambodia and the Sailendra in Malaysia.[25] The Hindus brought with them the concept of a God-King (Sanghyang Widi, the Supreme Being) who was worshipped in his many manifestations. Gradually the Balinese layered Agama Hinduism (worship of the manifestation of Siva, the destroyer) onto their native animism. Thus, by degrees already prosperous Bali became extensively Hindu by the year 1000.

This process was strengthened as the Singasari Empire rose in Eastern Java with its capital at Borobudur. It reached an apex when a Balinese noble, Udauama, married into the Singasari imperial family and became Emperor during the late Tenth and early Eleventh Centuries.

Not long afterward Singasari power declined allowing Balinese independence to flourish. Whenever this independence grew too great punitive expeditions were sent from Java to reinforce Balinese obedience. By the late Thirteenth Century the Majapahit Empire had risen to take over Java from the Singasari. After an expedition of conquest in 1343, Bali was made a dependent province. The province's ruler was called the Dewa Agung (Great Deity), a title that has endured through the centuries. Although this period produced 150 years of continued turbulence it didn't greatly affect either Balinese agricultural plenty or its basic societal structure.

In 1515 things began to change again. The Muslim Kingdom of Malacca overthrew the Majapahits and created the Maturam Empire centered on Java. The Majapahit royal family and chief followers fled to Bali. The age of a Hindu Bali counterposed to a Muslim Java had begun. So had the island's 'Golden Age'. With its capital at Gelgel on the South coast, Bali's 300,000 people were ruled by the great Batu Rengsong as Dewa Agung. He and his successors governed in increasing prosperity. The island, as well as the nearby islands of Lombok and Symbawa and parts of Eastern Java, were subject to centralized Balinese authority. There was a cultural renaissance, reviving the glittering Majapahit era. Trade was increased both to neighboring islands and the Asiatic mainland. The golden century lasted until 1639 when Matraram forces invaded successfully from East Java and temporarily ended Balinese independence. Through it all the island's villages and communities retained their strength, layering new customs and beliefs onto the traditional base.

Meanwhile, Europeans had found this productive paradise. The first to land probably was the Portuguese Fernando Mendez Pinto in 1546. While many explorers passed the island, including Sir Francis Drake in 1585, there are no records of landings until 1585, when the Dutch Captain Cornelis de Houtman arrived, staying long enough for one of his crew, Arnoudt Lintgens, to produce the first known map. By the early 1600s European contact had become regular, with the largest volume of trade carried by the newly created Netherlands East India Company.

What also had developed was Bali's 'Silver Age' which rose around a new capital, Klungkung, and lasted from 1650 to 1750. At this time the island became divided into twelve quasi independent rajadoms (of which eight still survive) which gradually absorbed the power, but not the title, of the Dewa Agung. Bali also asserted its independent power once again and expanded its control both to neighboring islands and to East Java. Balinese culture was inlaid with European imports, but the 'Silver Age' was essentially another Majapahit revival. Hinduism overlaying animism continued as the basic faithfaith.

As this age waned one of the rajadoms, Karangasem, began to assume control of the entire island. This started around 1800. But the Europeans had arrived in Southeast Asia in force and were not long content to leave Bali to its own devices. The Dutch, previously satisfied to be just traders, embarked upon a program of conquest in 1840. They conducted three campaigns against the heroic brother of the Raja of Karangasem, Gusti Ktut Jelantik. By 1850 the Dutch had defeated Gusti and his followers, many of whom had committed ritual suicide, but didn't crush all resistance until 1906. Following Dutch rule was the Japanese invasion of 1942, the independence of Indonesia from the Netherlands in 1952, and Bali's inclusion as part of the Republic of Indonesia in 1956. Since the rising, accompanying an attempted communist coup in 1965, which resulted in the massacre of about 100,000 Balinese, the island has ceased to bristle with fierce warriors and violence, becoming instead a haven for tourists interested in its beaches and culture.

The main point of this odyssey is to illustrate the numerous crisis and external transitions the island has undergone over the last 1500 years. Throughout all of them the fundamental social interactions and the culture have remained intact. Bali has endured as a coherent entity despite repeated conquests, disaster, and disease. In this it provides an example to be studied and emulated.

The sinews that have sustained the Balinese over the centuries are not surprising. They are community, tradition, family and faith. All flourish today. All are critical to the endurance of any culture or civilization.

Functional existence is built around the community, which in essence is the banjan, or a cooperative group of neighbors. Two or more banjan may inhabit a given village. In the fields the subak, an agricultural society to which individual plot owners belong, regulates the all-important distribution of water and attends other common needs. Its strength and proliferation has made the Balinese among the most efficient rice growers in Southeast Asia. Families, extended families, banjans and subaks, practice sharing, interaction, and cooperation over the entire spectrum of daily life set the societal tone.

Bali's religion, Agama Hinduism, involves not only worship of a supreme being with a destructive bent, it also involves delineation of an ordered, paired universe. The supernatural and unfathomable have practical participation in the myriad of regular tasks. Offerings, presented at the island's 30,000 temples (for 3 million inhabitants) or placed at the sites of specific activities, testify to continual religious relevance. So do the frequent ceremonies. The concept of pairing within the divine monad (good and evil, male and female, light and dark) is common to many belief systems. In its particular Balinese translation it enables believers to maintain a balanced outlook.[26] Everything contains another side, potentially emergent. There is less certainty, less egocentricity, and a greater sense of being humbled before a supreme power than exists in Bali's industrial counterparts.

Evidence of this duality and this humbling is contained in the Balinese belief that height is associated with holiness, which is exemplified by sacred but dangerously volcanic Mount Agurng with the island's primary temple nestled on its slopes at Besakih. In contrast, water, provider of much sustenance, is situated lower and represents evil. Mount Agung is an active volcano. Its most recent eruption was in March of 1963, eerily coincident with the most sacred of Balinese rituals, the Eka Dasa Rucha, held once every 100 years and centered on the Besakih temple. The festival had to be canceled, but although destruction was widespread the temple miraculously survived.[27] The Balinese are prepared to have tragedy emerge suddenly from placid piety. Nothing should be taken for granted. Evil can develop from good or good from evil. The land and its primal forces must always be placated and worshipped lest they turn hostile. This attitude has produced prosperity, dating from the beginning of recorded time.

In Hindu Bali many remnants of animism remain. One is the presence of leyaks, butas, and kalas. They are evil spirits who haunt the night, the woods, or the desolate coast, and need to be appeased or exorcised. Another is ancestor worship, a deeply rooted element of daily Balinese belief. Ancestors are a part of virtually every activity. The Hindu concept of three corporal elements fits nicely into this system. The first element, the material body, can be removed by the ceremony of cremation. The second, thought and feeling, constitute the intellectual and emotional element and also the element that engages in dream travel. The soul, the third element, is the being's essence and is never extinguished. It is freed by corporeal death to exist and participate in society. Ancestors are constantly present. The ability to interact with them at critical junctures and on celebratory occasions contributes significantly to the richness of Balinese communal life.

Beliefs, interaction, and a sense of community are heightened by the island's penchant for dance and drama, which are world famous[28]. Families participate together. So do larger communal groups. This helps preserve ties as well as express feelings. Together the pillars of Balinese society have survived repeated turmoil, natural disaster, and thus far even the encroachments of the modern world. In its prosperity and sophistication the island has changed little since the days of animism. This has happened because its people never strayed too far from the humility of their spiritual and communal roots.

Australia's Aboriginals like the Bushmen of the Kalahari are basically hunter-gatherers. Similarly the Aboriginals have a social and belief structure that is far more complex than it appears at first glance.

This ancient people has viscerally understood, since its migration from Southeast Asia at least 46,000 years ago,[29] that survival depends upon sharing, upon family, upon community and, above all, upon veneration of the land. This knowledge is combined with a high degree of intelligence that manifests itself in a myriad of ways, such as linguistic ability and art. Together these attributes have enabled Aboriginals to survive as a society under conditions that might have eradicated most cultures.

Aboriginal social construction is founded upon a creation myth, the Dreaming, that directly connects its history with the present, and permeates every aspect of daily life. "The concept of the Dreaming refers to the ancestral past, to the Ancestral Beings' itinerary of travel across the landscape, and to dreams themselves in which sequences of the ancestral past are revealed. But the Dreaming is also the sacred dimension of the present, the driving force that Aborigines believe underlies the here and now...Today Aboriginal people see direct continuity between the ancestral past, their landscape, and themselves. They see the landscape as alive with the power of the ancestors and, at the same time, humanized in its essential oneness with the living."[30] With this credo they bear kinship with many native peoples the world over who have a perspective that differs markedly from the shallow immediacy of the industrialized nations.

The Dreaming does something else equally significant. It binds each inhabitant closely to the land. "Aboriginal creation myths tell of the legendary totemic beings who wandered over the continent in the Dreamtime, singing out the name of everything that crossed their path - birds, animals, plants, rocks, water holes - and so singing the world into existence."[31] Each individual identifies a particular totemic being. Each present and totemic being has its own collection of sacred sites and their attendant songlines cataloguing its wanderings. Knowledge of the past and responsibility for the songlines is each individual's sacred trust. It is deeply felt that, "an unsung land is a dead land: since, if the songs are forgotten, the land itself will die."[32] Thus the people, their past and their land are tightly welded, their existences inseparable.

One of the most important concepts inculcated into Aboriginal society is that of sharing. Sharing goes much deeper than the basic knowledge that survival might depend upon its enactment. It covers not only food and shelter, but the entire system of beliefs and 'ownership' of the songlines lacing the land's surface. "White men made the common mistake of assuming that because the Aboriginals were wanderers they could have no system of land tenure. This was nonsense. Aboriginals, it was true, could not imagine territory as a block of land hemmed in by frontiers; but rather as an interlocking network of 'lines' or 'ways through'."[33] These songlines, and their dependent territory are shared. Neighbors exchange responsibility for access to both the song and the territory which fosters communication and ensures protection. Throughout history most Aboriginals have learned to speak several of their more than 200 separate languages (of which only 12 survive[34]) in order to more freely exchange obligations with kindred peoples. Individual responsibility for specific myths and locations along the various songlines create a sort of shared tenancy with a definite etiquette governing traversal with proper respect. This system seems to have drawn the various Aboriginal people closer together with a commonly expressed media of interaction. In the Aboriginal view, "music is a memory bank for finding one's way about the world".[35] The songlines are the highways through the landscape of each others' history, as well as the governors of daily life.

As with many peoples the extended family is the basic Aboriginal functional entity. Above that sit the totemic corporations whose sets of people usually bisect family lines, giving them extended reach as well as interdependence. Tribal and linguistic groups encompass larger numbers, but are also bound to each other by the web of interlocking beliefs. In essence, all of Aboriginal society is structured not only for survival but also for harmony and equality.

In many areas, such as language, government, beliefs and art, this seemingly simple hunter-gatherer culture reveals a subcutaneous sophistication and innate intelligence that is dazzlingly modern. Supporting this intricate structure is a fundamental unity. "In traditional Aboriginal thought, there is no central dichotomy of the spiritual and material, the sacred and the secular, or the natural and the supernatural."[36] This unity lends a large degree of power to each element of individual existence. That power with its ancestral wellspring courses through a single representational aorta, the songlines, making beliefs all the more able to energize and direct society.

In addition to unity, Aboriginal society is balanced. "An emphasis on symmetry in this aesthetic tradition matches the profound strains of balanced dualism, reciprocity and equality that underlie the intellectual framework of so many Aboriginal social institutions and their cultural emblems, especially those associated with marriage."[37] Everything in life strives for balance, punctuated by equality. Senses are tuned to react quickly to any evidence of disequilibrium, whether it be overuse of the land or lack of proper regard for a songline. By way of comparison, it is interesting that the 'original intent' of those that founded democratic republicanism in the United States was also based upon achieving governmental balance and equilibrium.

A profound reverence for ancestors is reinforced by being woven together with respect for elders. Tradition, history, and wisdom are all employed daily via this principle. Over the years of Aboriginal existence, "law and order was maintained through the infusion of religious ideology into everyday actions and through enforcement by senior men and women."[38] This has bound together the principles of unity with age and ancestors as a societal anchor to windward. The youth-oriented, technological societies of today have cut loose such anchors, to their great detriment.

A well constructed foundation has enabled the Aboriginals to withstand repeated waves of cultural shock that would have brought most societies to their knees. It has allowed a sense of identity to persist. It has provided beacons for perseverance that industrial/technological nations would be wise to heed.

There is an additional critical factor - expression and its ramifications. "The imagery of Aboriginal art, and that of the songs, dances, and ceremonial paraphernalia, is related both to the past bodies of Aboriginal mythic narrative and to the wider symbolisms of daily life and belief. Together these symbolisms constitute a complex code of interaction that continually remodels, and at the same time reflects, Aboriginal cosmology, sociality, and notions of the person."[39] What serves a similar role in technological societies? Television? Music videos? Computers? What sets their code of interaction? What guidelines from the past do they employ? What traditions do they venerate? While there are obviously some valuable forms of expression in technological nations, there is little any longer that provides the strong cultural mortar still created by the Aboriginals.

It is a main contention of this book that those very elements of our industrial/technological world that have long been dismissed as hopelessly primitive may actually contain the precepts that can return us to the bedrock that can rescue us. Whatever these 'advanced' nations eventually choose to do, the civilizations of the coming century are likely to be built upon the solidity of these enduring precepts. Family, community, ancestors, and faith will be their supporting pillars. In this fundamental aspect the new civilizations are likely to bear more resemblance to the four examples noted above than to the industrial/technological societies of today's First World.

---

1 Paul Johnson, *Modern Times* (Harper Perennial, NY, 1992) p. 784.

2 Robert Moss, "We Are All Related," *Parade Magazine,* Oct. 11, 1992

3 Hans-Joachim Heinz and Marshall Lee, *Namkwa: Life Among the Bushmen* (Houghton Mifflin Company, Boston, 1979) p. 197.

4 sometimes called the San

5 Noël Mostert, *Frontiers* (Alfred A. Knopf, NY, 1992) p. 24.

6 The average Bushwoman, responsible for food collection, will be able to recognize at least 300 plants in whatever configuration they might appear.

7 Hans-Joachim Heinz and Marshall Lee, *Namkwa: Life Among the Bushmen* (Houghton Mifflin Company, Boston ,1979) p. 58.

8 Researchers have estimated that infants are carried almost 5,000 miles before they are required to walk.

9 Hans-Joachim Heinz and Marshall Lee, *Namkwa: Life Among the Bushmen* (Houghton Mifflin Company, Boston, 1979) p. 85.

10 Ibid., p. 1230.

11 Noël Mostert, *Frontiers* (Alfred A. Knopf) p. 29.

12 L.S. Stavriamos, *The Promise of the Coming Dark Age* (W.H. Freeman and Company, San Francisco, 1976) p. 165.

13 Michael D. Coe, *The Maya* (Thames & Hudson Ltd., London ,1966)

14 The Maya number system was very simple. It employed only three symbols: a dot with the value of one; a horizontal bar for five and a shell-

like symbol signifying zero or completed. Thus numerals up to four could be represented by dots. Nineteen was the highest coefficient in the calendar and was four dots above three bars. Written numbers were vejesimal increasing from bottom to top in vertical columns. The first and lowest place had a value of one, the next above it 20, then 400.

[15] Although they understood the concept of the wheel, and incorporated in their children's playthings, they did not utilize it due largely to absence of draft animals.

[16] John S. Henderson, *The World of the Ancient Maya* (Cornell University Press, Ithaca, 1981) p. 198.

[17] Linda Schele and David Freidell, *A Forest of Kings - The Untold Story of the Ancient Maya* (William Morrow & Company, Inc., NY, 1990) p. 392. The last recorded Late Classic date, June 20, 909 was found carved on a tree-stone at Tonina in Mexico's Chiapas highlands.

[18] Rigoberto Menchú, *I Rigoberto Menchú - An Indian Woman in Guatemala,* ed. and intro. Elizabeth Burgos-DeGray, trans. Ann Wright, (Verso, London, 1984) p. 80.

[19] The Maya calendar starts with the meshing of a 260 day year (13, 20 day months) with a separately named 360 day solar year (18, 20 day months and 5 unlucky days at year end). Each day had a name provided by a combination of 260 and 360 day nomenclatures at the given point of juncture. The Calendar Round is 52 years, the time it would take for any particular one of the named days to recur. The long count was based upon the 360 day solar year. It used combinations of 20, 20 day months (360 days, 7,200 days, 144,000 days) as its basic points of reference. This Long Count stretched back to a specific date, 13 August 3114 BC (in the Georgian calendar) cited as the Maya historical beginning.

[20] Rigoberto Menchú, *I Rigoberto Menchú - An Indian Woman in Guatemala,* ed. and intro. Elizabeth Burgos-DeGray, trans. Ann Wright, (Verso, London, 1984) p. 57.

[21] Ibid., p. 43.

[22] Ibid., p. 49.

[23] Lorraine Stobbart, *Utopia Fact or Fiction, The Evidence From the Americas* (Alan Sutton Publishing, London, 1992) p. 122.

[24] Miguel Covarrubias, *Island of Bali* (Alfred A. Knopf, NY, 1936).

[25] R.C. Majumdar, H.C. Raychudhuri, *An Advanced History of India* (Kalikinkar Data, MacMillan & Co. Ltd, London, 1958).

[26] ed. W.F. Wertheim, *Bali; Studies in Life, Thought and Ritual* (The Royal Tropical Institute, Amsterdam, 1960).

[27] Anna Mathews, *The Night of Prunama* (Jonathan Cape, London, 1965).

[28] de Zoete, Beryl, Spies, *Dance and Drama in Bali* (Faber & Faber, London, 1938).

[29] A.A. Abbie, *The Original Austrailians* (Frederick Muller, London, 1969).

[30] Bruce Chatwin, *The Songlines* (Penguin Books, London, 1988) p. 2.
[31] ed. Peter Sutton, *Dreamings: The Art of Aboriginal Austrailia* (The Asia Society of New York in Association with George Brazil Publishers, 1988).
[32] Bruce Chatwin, *The Songlines* (Penguin Books, London, 1988) p. 52.
[33] Ibid., p. 56.
[34] F. Bobes, *Race, Language, and Culture* (Macmillan, NY 1896).
[35] Bruce Chatwin, *The Songlines* (Penguin Books, London, 1988) p. 108.
[36] ed. Peter Sutton, *Dreamings: The Art of Aboriginal Austrailia* (The Asia Society of New York in Association with George Brazil Publishers, 1988) p. 16.
[37] Ibid., p. 7.
[38] Ibid.
[39] Ibid., p. 14.

CHAPTER 10

Fundamental Values and Structures

In this section four societies have been examined. They are merely representative of many that dot the globe. They were selected because in their midst the elements necessary to fuel the growth of new civilizations clearly seem to flourish. They exemplify the retention of necessary basics in the confusion of our modern world. It is likely that the vital roots of family, community, tradition, and faith will thrust most powerfully from the fecundity of Third World environments.

Industrial/technological societies are not unaware that these key civilizational ingredients are disintegrating beneath them. While remaining pledged to 'growth' and 'progress' they are attempting to shore up their crumblin' foundations. Some of the terms that are being reiterated today, reflecting the various aspects of this effort, are 'Family values', 'nurturing rights', 'Founding Fathers" and 'moral majority'. Michael Lerner is not alone in, "recognizing that human beings have a fundamental need to be part of communities of spiritual and ethical meaning and purpose that transcend the individual, we are drawn immediately to look at the two main arenas in which most people spend the majority of their time in adult life: work and family. . .If you re-establish a sense of community and undermine the self-blaming that tends to go along with breakdowns of social support, you could increase health and productivity as well as bolster family ties."[1] He is only one of many echoing similar sentiments.

However, what comes naturally in much of the Third World has to be manufactured in the First. Old habits have been discontinued. Extended families are no longer recognizable. Communities are hard to identify. Tradition has been displaced. The task of regeneration is made all the more onerous in societies encumbered by attachment to baggage such as individual rights and sybaritic living standards. While both may enhance the ambiance of daily existence, they also sap the energy needed to create and expand civilizations. Bertrand Russell accurately observed that, "in general, important civilizations start with a rigid and superstitious system"[2]. These characteristics no longer apply to the First World.

A CACOPHONY OF CONTRASTS

The First and Third Worlds project very different images and consequently possess very different futures. The reverberations from their clashes resound throughout the globe. The First World is marshaling its resources in a struggle to maintain an established, and expected, living standard. Conversely, the Third is seeking to rise above subsistence by increasing societal tensile strength. The contrasts in method and direction are significant.

In the industrial/technological nations, "the task for the future is to replace the longing for imaginary community with a communal imagination that is part of government."[3] They are enduring the loss of emotional anchors to windward, such as family and community, brought on by a deluge of technological individualism. This has led to attempts to recreate basic societal components whose obliteration is already well advanced and whose forms are often unrecognizable. Zbignew Brzezinski comments that, "the priority given to individual self-gratification combined with the growing capacity of the human being to reshape itself through genetic and other forms of scientific self-alteration, with neither subject to mutual restraint, tend to create a condition in which little self control is exercised over the dynamics of the desire to consume and to tinker with the self."[4] It is this compulsion that has largely erased the fundamental institutional outlines and necessitated the task of their reinvention. The compulsion goes even further. The West's entire existence is now at risk. "Only hubris can explain why so many Western societies are trying to defy the economic laws of gravity. Budgetary discipline is disappearing. Extensive social programs and pork-barrel projects multiply with little heed to costs. The West's savings and investment rates lead to declining competitiveness vis-a-vis East Asia. The work ethic is eroding, while politicians delude workers into believing that they can retain high wages despite becoming internationally uncompetitive. Leadership is lacking."[5] This is the economic crisis in a nutshell. Its severity has increased the danger from problems in other areas: social, environmental, psychological, theological, and governmental.

Third World societies, on the other hand, are closer to the allegiances developed under the rigors of subsistence living. They are described by Nöel Mostert. "What was important, as in all other aspects of the Xhosa social code, was that the wholeness of the family, the chiefdom, and the society be preserved, and there was no frailty of the flesh, or even serious misdemeanor, that was larger than the overwhelming instinct for maintaining the balances in their long-established social harmonies."[6] Social harmonies - two words highlight both the essence of these Third World peoples and the critical differences between them and those industrial/technological nations primarily concerned with individual rights, their expressions, and their possessions. The former has the potential for building civilizational strength. The latter must expend most of their energy to keep them from unraveling.

Lifestyles are also very different. Most industrial nations are generally living above their means, but determined to persist in doing so. Massive energy inputs, consumer electronics, exotic vacations, and extensive wardrobes are only some of the components that wed these nations to irrational destructive profligacy. In many Third World nations things tend to be simpler. Survival is more of an issue. The pursuit of 'progress' hasn't yet gotten out of hand. Communal allegiances tend to be stronger. The cement of faith hasn't yet begun to crack and chip. Caroline Hebard, who travels the world with her dogs performing rescues, has observed first hand. "One thing I've learned is that there are an awful lot of good people around. And I think that, in some ways, the simpler they are, the less well-off, the more they will reach out to others. The less cluttered with material and egotistical aspects of life they are, the more caring they will be."[7] This matters in trying to build societies or sustain civilizations. The focus of simplicity has been gained and lost repeatedly. It is one reason why civilizations rise and fall. However pleasant it might feel to be encrusted with materialism and options, it is not a good recipe for civilizational vitality.

Faith is another divide, The laser-like parity of belief builds and transmits civilizational energy. Individualism, apathy, and agnosticism diffuse it. In the First World the latter condition has prevailed, even deepened. "For four centuries, every man has not only been his own priest, but also his own professor of ethics, and the consequence is an anarchy which threatens that minimum consensus of value necessary to the political state."[8] In the Third World faith tends to be alive in everyday existence, or throbbing very near the surface. The intensity of unquestioning devotion can often be ridiculed, or feared, by the supposedly more sophisticated. But it has always been that necessary binder that secures a civilization's building blocks.

Another characteristic found in the more industrial, technological societies is an increasingly shorter term outlook. Sometimes the impetus is political. At other times it is material Often it is egocentric. Whatever the cause, the fact is inescapable and with it has come the gradual withering of our collective past. Henry James, as described by Paul Johnson, understood how precious the past could be. "For him, history, tradition, precedence, and established forms constituted the inherited wisdom of civilization, the only reliable guides to human behavior."[9]

What has the First World created instead as its behavior guides? Television and radio talk shows, soap operas, and music videos are its myths. Science fiction, video games, and romance novels comprise its imagination. Its collective soul and its conscience have been swallowed by technology and greed. Despite the many material benefits it provided, capitalism fractured families along fault lines of gender and generation by demanding for market production the male labor traditionally devoted to family, subsistence and reproduction."[10] Holistic thought patterns, communal institutions, traditions, faith - the soul of any civilization - have been gradually displaced by devotion to individualism an the production of material goods. This is less true in the Third World although we are attempting to change that through the temptations of materialism. Soul-producing qualities still flourish in many places, and, where absent, their flames can be rekindled more easily. It is a virtual certainty that in the civilizations of the future the individualistic and characteristics of democracy and capitalism will play a much smaller role than they do in the West today, and that the institutions of family, community, tradition, and faith will once again rise to a more prominent position.

VIRULENT BREEDING GROUNDS

The vast swamps of the world's disadvantaged have grown larger and relatively less prosperous in the post-World War II half-century.

They have become breeding grounds for those who have less and less to lose. These people have an increasing incentive to change the existing systems. They live in the South Bronx and in Calcutta. The scramble for survival in the hills of Chiapas and the desert of Chad. Here and there among them new civilizations are incubating.

By most estimates there are over 1 billion people (out of the world's 5.5 billion) who live below the United Nations' determined subsistence poverty level. There are 2 billion more who are barely above the income levels needed to survive. The explosive population growth projected to take place over the next twenty-five to thirty years, which will bring the world total up to 8 billion, will largely occur among these extremely disadvantaged. Increasingly these individuals will dwell in urban slums. Even given recent economic successes like Singapore, Chile, Taiwan and South Korea, or apparent political successes like South Africa, Nicaragua, and Hungary, the plight of the poor is deepening, relatively, on all fronts. Those in rural areas are streaming to the cities, hoping for the sustenance previously denied them. They are particularly volatile. They are prepared to undergo any sacrifice for the sake of future generations. They are the approaching wave.

It is when people have little to lose, or when they are scarred by envy and resentment, that they become most dangerous to established systems. It seems evident that the spread of Marxism through the Third World came not primarily from ideological affinity, or even understanding, it was adopted as an expression of frustration, of envy, of yearning. The previous system had not worked. Adherence to colonial or post-colonial norms would have at best produced a gradually trained and educated elite which might eventually have provided solid national economics and political entities as advertised. Marxism and socialism promised immediate equality. It turned out to be a false promise, as many in the West predicted at the time. That Marxist economics was overly simplistic, unsound, and prone to dictatorial abuse was beside the point. Those among the deprived that were under the colonial yoke were promised immediate hope. The same desperate conditions are widespread in the Third World today. The fruits of democracy and capitalism are either far removed or only available to an elite. The mass of Third World residents crammed into the squalor of urban tenements have little prospect of such attainment. They are susceptible to egalitarian doctrine which seems simple, powerful, and immediate. Former communists had the same susceptibility and grasped at the straws of democracy and free markets without estimating the required price.

There are other doctrines waiting to snare them. "The success of Islamic Fundamentalists in Egypt has been due in part to their ability to channel public discontent with the economy into support for an Islamic Regime."[11] This is also the source of popularity for rampant anti-Americanism, although, "a more traditional Islamic Arab world does not have to be a more anti-American one, unless the United States helps to make that happen."[12] At a time when the triumph of capitalism and democracy appears assured and complete, and when United States power seems to straddle the globe, all three are actually at their most fragile point in the last fifty years. The number of people with an interest in promoting alternatives is growing. Remedies for the world's problems, emerging from the capitalistic democratic systems as practiced, are shrinking.

As hope turns to envy, and then despair, among the disadvantaged multitudes the eventual nature of politics will take shape. Nationalism is not likely to prove significant, as its current manifestations suggest. "Nationalism - an identification with the life and aspirations of uncounted millions whom we shall never know, with a territory we shall never visit in its entirety - is qualitatively different from the love of family or of home surroundings."[13] If not nations, then what? There are likely to be two emergences - one smaller, one larger. On the one hand families and communities will become even more important. There will be a price, for this audit will be demand forfeiture of some individual freedoms. "No fundamental strengthening of community life will be possible unless individuals give back certain of their rights to communities, and accept the return of certain historical forms of intolerance."[14] This will be far easier to accomplish in the Third World than in the First. It will lead to more structure, more intolerance, more social rigidity as a trade off for purpose, pride, and the promise of accomplishments. In the Third World the trade off will seem more advantageous due to present imbalances.

The other emergence will be supranational. It will be religious. It will be economic. It will be ethnic. It will be all of the above, and more, depending on the time and the place. The engines of the new civilizations are likely to combine, as did many of their predecessors, the dream of egalitarianism with the practical illusions of authoritarianism.

NASCENT DYNAMISM

The new civilizational energy may well come boiling up from the Third World wasteland, in an essentially egalitarian, primarily authoritarian format. This will occur, as Alfred Kazin noted, due to the enervation of the First World. "What has not remained anywhere is the 'utopian' drive and confidence in the future that sparked the early 20th century. We live in an age of unparalleled technological power and scientific advance, but the spirit is tired, political authority is discredited, civic violence is on a mass scale, race relations are at their worst in the vast underclass, public education is a catastrophe; the general dependence on commercial television sets the tone, the speech, the morale of national life toward an irreversible mediocrity...narcissism is our reigning ideology."[15] An opportunity for charismatic leaders, religious fervor, and powerful doctrine has been created by the collapse of the developed nations' societal strength. It has been created by a reservoir of human beings whose future is dimming daily and whose resentment is building. It has been created by a military build-up, particularly in Asia, of frightening proportions, which has placed armed might in the hands of many with the most severe resentments. Finally, it has been created by coagulation in industrial nations where gridlock and cries to 'do something' have begun to overcome the taste for democratic government.

As the coming century progresses it is likely that the Third World, at the same time that is growing more egalitarian and authoritarian, will adapt some of the industrial nations' procedures and technology to fit its own requirements. One of these could be more labor intensive than capital intensive industry, such as that advocated by Mahatma Ghandi fifty years ago. Another could be new financial systems, incorporating innovations designed for the relatively disadvantaged, such as the peer lending now employed in Bangladesh. New economics and government designed to provide meaning and sustenance to a wider array of individuals. This could permit reinvigoration of areas that now appear moribund. This will be dynamic, but it will require rigidity of social and governmental structure.

For all its accomplishments and prowess the First World has lost its confidence. It is increasingly shrinking from conflict. It is progressively evading its internal patterns. It is merely seeking to safeguard the status quo. New civilizations have yet to exhibit their own momentum and personality. But as they coalesce and grow their confidence will build. "There is no better instance of how a burst of civilization depends on confidence than the Florentine state of mind in the early fifteenth-century."[16] Fundamental Islamic confidence is growing. So is that of the Chinese. Latin America is developing confidence as well. Others are emerging. The new civilizations will be drawn from their ranks.

What has happened in the Industrial World is that the 'haves', in their rush to protect possessions and life styles, have forgotten the needs of ordinary human beings. This is true in their own countries and elsewhere. They have abandoned the principles of their origins and their sense of purpose for defensiveness. The senses of mission and of risk taking, which constitute civilizational dynamics, have atrophied. Presently they will reappear, transferred to new entities whose fundamentals are intact.

President Woodrow Wilson of the United States understood. "When I survey the genesis of America I see this written on every page: that the nations are renewed from the bottom, not the top; that the genius which springs up from the ranks of unknown men is the genius which renews the youth and energy of a people. Everything I know about history, every bit of experience and observation that has contributed to my thought, has confirmed me in the conviction that the real wisdom of human life is compounded out of the experiences of ordinary men. The utility, the vitality, the fruitage of life does not come from the top to the bottom; it comes, like the natural growth of a great tree, from the soil, up through the trunk into the branches, to the foliage and the fruit. The great struggling unknown masses of the men who are at the base of everything are the dynamic force that is lifting the level of society. A nation is as great, and only as great, as her rank and file."[17] The ordinary, unknown masses waiting to transmit the fruitage of life, beginning to capture the dynamic force of civilization, currently lie outside the First World. The central kernel of their dynamism carries more than a hint of tribal energy. It would be prudent for us in the industrial/technological nations to heed the sources of this energy. It is evening, but not yet too late for us to adapt before we are surrounded, and then engulfed.

---

1 Michael Lerner, *TIKKIN* magazine Vol. 8, No. 3, p. 24.

2 Bertrand Russell, *A History of Western Philosophy* (Simon and Schuster, NY, 1945) p. XXIII.

3 James A. Morone, *The Democratic Wish* (Basic Books, 1990) p. 30.

4 Zbignew Brezinski, *Out of Control - Global Turmoil on the Eve of the 21st Century* (Charles Scribner's & Sons, NY, 1993) p. XII.

5 Kishnore Mahbubani, "The Dangers of Decadence," *Foreign Affairs*, Vol. 72, No. 4, Sept./Oct. 1993, p. 14.

6 Nöel Mostert, *Frontiers* (Alfred A. Knopf, NY, 1992) p. 958.

7 *Parade Magazine*, Sept. 12, 1993, p. 6.

[8] Richard Weaver, *Ideas Have Consequences* (University of Chicago Press, 1948) p. 3.

[9] Paul Johnson, *The Intellectuals* (Harper Collins, NY, 1988) p. 242.

[10] Charles Sellars, *Market Revolution* (Oxford University Press, 1991) p. 252.

[11] "The Battle for Egypt" *Foreign Affairs* Vol. 72, No. 4, Sept./Oct. 1993, p. 97.

[12] Ibid., p. 107.

[13] Hans Kohn, *The Idea of Nationalism: A Study of Its Origins and Background* (MacMillan, Toronto, 1967) p. 9.

[14] Francis Fukuyama, *The End of History and the Last Man* (The Free Press, NY, 1992) p. 326.

[15] Alfred Kazin, "Cry, the Beloved Country," *Forbes*, September 14, 1992, p. 156.

[16] Kenneth Clark, *Civilization* (Harper Perennials, NY, 1969) p. 89.

[17] Woodrow Wilson, *The New Freedom* (New York ,1913) pp 79-80.

PART IV

Tesserae of the Emerging Mosaic

"The collapse of communism does not guarantee the permanent universal triumph of capitalism and democracy. We must remember what gave birth to communism in the first place: the social upheavals and new poverty brought about by the Industrial Revolution, troubles that preceded its immense benefits. The man-made calamities of the capitalistic free market constituted, as it were, acts of God without God. The socialist movements that sprang up in protest were animated partly by Luddite rage, partly by the dreams of a just and stable society, a New Jerusalem. These dreams have not been eradicated by their devastating practical failure."

Henry Grunwald
"The Year 2000: Is It the End - or Just the Beginning?"
Time Magazine, March 30, 1992

CHAPTER 11

The Evolution of Socio-Politics

As an important calendric event approaches with the century's end there are new civilizations on the horizon. Perhaps they can be recognized in advance. At the very least many of their tendencies and components can be identified and explored.

Before so doing it would be useful to clarify the difference between opinions and predications. Many of the former have been offered thus far. More are due. Predictions, on the other hand, imply regularity and certainty. The world contains little of that.

A brief glance at cycles and rhythms may serve to illustrate. The word cycle is derived from the Greek word for circle which means, "coming around again to the place of beginning". It does not imply that there is a regular period of time before returning to the start. Rhythm is derived from the Greek word for measured time, and implies a regular interval of time. Historic probabilities can often have a cyclic quality. They do not have a discernible rhythm. Hence, peering into the future involves grappling with probabilities and arriving at opinions, not identifying certainties and making predictions.

Judge Learned Hand, commenting on the qualities demanded of judges, identified one further bridge between history, the present and the future. "A judge, in order to preserve his authority, and the authority of his decisions, must wrap himself in the mantle of the past...But at the same time he must find an accommodation with the dominant needs of his times."[1] The first task has been to uncover the mantle of the past, so often neglected in this world of immediacy. The next task is to determine what are the needs of our times. The multitudes of disadvantaged with their lives of little promise may well determine the texture of the world's future for us. Their needs, rather than the accomplishments of the 'haves', are likely to control the socio-political systems of the next century. We must initially explore which of their needs will be dominant and how they will be manifested? After that we should try to discover how the industrial/technological nations can best position themselves to respond to these needs and thus preserve the vitality of their civilization. The final question, the one for the next chapter, is to ask, given human nature and societal inertia, what is likely to happen?

We must try to translate attitudes into potential political expressions. We must try to see which of these expressions could become important civilizational components.

Our primary thesis has been that, "one coherent world system which has developed at a leisurely pace is going into or completing its decline, while another system is being born amid much hesitation and decay."[2] Can we identify this new system, or systems? Our approach is to inspect three potential socio-political systems as the keystone tesserae of the emerging mosaic.

EGALITARIAN AUTHORITARIANISM

There are two basic impulses that impel people to accept egalitarian authoritarianism. The first is the desire to share in both opportunity and reward. This desire emerged from the distant marches of history and was articulated by the Greek philosophers. Since the Eighteenth Century it has served as a basis for both democracy and socialism. The second impulse is the urge 'to get things done'. Periodic gridlock and inefficiency have plagued every form of government yet devised. Not surprisingly the rise of powerful individuals has usually coincided with crisis and inaction. Whether it be Pericles, who unified and dominated ancient Athens to create its Golden Age, or Mussolini once lauded for 'making the trains run on time', it is an historical fact that bestowal of authority can often be seductively attached to timely oiling of the wheels of government and production of significant achievements. Realization that the strictures of absolute power can be confining to individual lifestyles comes later, usually too late to temper the exercise of authority.

Those people in disadvantaged circumstances throughout the world, are vulnerable to these two impulses. Most have little to lose by creating strong authority. Unfortunately for the First World, many agree with Christopher Lasch that, "the need for a more equitable distribution of wealth ought to be obvious, both on moral and on economic grounds, and it cannot be achieved under an advanced system of capitalist production...equality implies a recognition of limits."[3] Despite pockets of achievement, the majority of people in the Third World are becoming increasingly disillusioned. In many cases they believe that they have not even received the scraps from the capitalists' table, and collectively have continued to slip farther behind economically. For example, both the Human Development Index compiled by the United Nations and the Human Suffering Index compiled by the Population Crisis Committee show gaps widening over the last twenty years between richer and poorer nations. This gapping is not confined to the Third World. Even within industrial/technological nations poverty has deepened in many cases. For instance, the United States Census Bureau reported that in 1992 the number of people living below the poverty line increased to 36.9 million, or 14.5 percent of the total population. The highest percentage since 1962.

What does this portend? In a world where the wealthier, industrialized nations are increasingly strapped financially, their capacity to aid the less fortunate is decreasing. With population surging among poorer peoples (partly due to medical advances provided by technology) the ranks of the disadvantaged are likely to swell over the next decades. Deprivation and envy will create hostility to a system which appears to produce wealthy, powerful elites both among nations and within nations. Thus, the majority of the world's population is likely to view the democratic, free market system of the First World with increasing suspicion and antipathy. The pressure for egalitarianism will likely come from these disadvantaged. It is likely to intensify.

The world is faced with complex problems. Democratic governments are not by nature good problem solvers. The world's democratic model, the United States, is a good illustration. Its constitution was written with the intent to create governmental balance. This effort was more concerned with limiting the power of each branch relative to the other than it was with creating a problem solving mechanism. Its evolution has been characterized much more by compromise than decisiveness; protection of rights rather than fluidity or action. While this system has worked reasonably well for United State citizens over their first two hundred years, it has gradually produced governmental gridlock so encrusted with bureaucracy that motion toward problem solving is glacial. Even citizens of the United States and its First World compatriots are growing frustrated with governmental impotence. With the demands to 'do something' resounding from even the most democratic nations, the progression towards bigger, more invasive, and more authoritarian government is well underway. Receptivity is growing almost everywhere in the world to charismatic authoritarian leadership promising decisive action. The odds in favor of authoritarianism's appearance in more locations over the next few decades are escalating.

Prime candidates for the installations of egalitarian authoritarian regimes fall into two categories. The first is nations where resentment against capitalistic elitism is the strongest, primarily for economic reasons. Good examples of this category are places where the several varieties of Fundamental Islam flourishes. Islamic fundamentalism is a virulent and contagious expression of an egalitarian desire. It depends upon rigid central authority. It is likely to spread rapidly among the Muslim disadvantaged.

The other type of nation particularly susceptible to egalitarian authoritarianism is one where nostalgic memories of past glories are heightened by current economic and political chaos. A good example of this is Russia. Given its history and its impatience with the process of establishing democracy and free markets, institution of an authoritarian government with egalitarian pretensions appears not to be far in the future.

Egalitarian authoritarianism is well placed to handle the dynamics of new civilizations. It holds out the promise of both equality and action and can readily channel energy. Whether religious or political in nature, egalitarian authoritarianism is likely to play an important role during the next century.

HAVELIAN CONSCIENCE POLITICS

This political expression represents more of a hope than a likelihood. If the key elements of Western civilization are to revitalize themselves, if there is to be a continuation of the American age, something akin to Conscience Politics will have to develop.

Václav Havel is one of the great governmental philosophers of all time. He resembles a present day Thomas Jefferson or James Madison in his ability to articulate the rights and obligations of individuals within a political system. The essence of his philosophy is contained in two essays: "Politics and Conscience" and "The Power of the Powerless," and a paragraph from the former sums up Havel's ideals.

"The question is wholly other, deeper, and equally relevant to all; whether we shall, by whatever means, succeed in reconstituting the natural world as the true terrain of politics, rehabilitating the personal experience of human beings as the initial measure of things, placing morality above politics and responsibility above our desires, in making human community meaningful, in retaining content to human speech, in reconstituting, as the focus of all social action, the autonomous, integral and dignified human 'I', responsible for ourselves because we are bound to something higher, and capable of sacrificing something, in extreme cases even everything, of his banal, prosperous private life - that 'rule of everydayness' as Jan Patocka used to say - for the sake of that which gives life meaning."[4]

Havel wrote these words in February, 1984 as part of a speech to be delivered in acceptance of an honorary doctorate from the University of Toulouse in May of that year. He was not allowed to travel and deliver it in person, being restricted by the then communist regime of Czechoslovakia. What he has to say constitutes the critical challenge for the industrial/technological nations of the First World. If their civilization is to persist, and to attain greater influence, something similar to the principles articulated by Havel needs to emerge from the ethical and economic miasma that currently prevails. The pivotal question is whether the nations possess the means and the will to effect such a transformation. In theory the process could be simple, involving a change in individual attitudes. In reality it will prove much more complex.

The means to develop different perspectives are clearly present. The will is more difficult to determine. One way to measure it is to look at what is taking place in those urban metropoli which contain both the majority of the industrial/technological nations' population and their most oppressive social problems.

First we should define what Havel means by "Natural World" and see how is applies to cities, and ultimately civilizations. "Politics and Conscience," defines it fundamentally. "Our 'I' primordially attests to that world and personally certifies it; that is the world of our lived experience...in this world, categories like justice, honor, treason, friendship, infidelity, courage, or empathy have a wholly tangible content, relating to actual persons and important for actual life." This world of personal experience is finite and limited. "The natural world, in virtue of its very being, bears with it the presupposition of the absolute which grounds, delimits, animates and directs it... Any attempt to spurn it, master it, or replace it with something else, appears, within the framework of the natural world, as an expression of hubris from which humans must pay a heavy price...Human beings must pay a heavy price for every attempt to abolish, radically, once for all and without a trace, that humbly respected boundary of the natural world, with its tradition of scrupulous personal acknowledgment. They must pay for the attempt to seize nature, to leave not a remnant of it in human hands, to ridicule its mystery; they must pay for the attempt to abolish God and play at being God...the fault is not one of science as such but of the arrogance of man in the age of science. Man is simply not God, and playing God has cruel consequences." In Havel's eyes we are guilty of trying to subvert the Natural World and replace it with egocentric elitism.

These consequences are tragically evident in inner cities. Obviously urban squalor is by no means unique to the modern age. What is unique is its relative importance. Never before has the world's overall population and living style been so affected by the condition of its cities. The trends are in place to increase this impact. How bad is it now? We can judge for ourselves. Are crime, drugs, violence, poverty, and homelessness diminishing? Are effective programs in place to alleviate these blights and improve inner city health, education, housing, and employment? Has the industrial/technological world come to grips with the complexities of its environmental, sociological, and economic challenges, as they apply to its urban areas? Most people would reply in the negative to all of the above questions. Inner cities, or whole cities for that matter, cannot be walled off from available resources and ignored by the populace. That will only allow the cancer to spread. The sole cure is decisive remedial action, enacted with a high priority.

The plight of large cities is in many ways desperate. There isn't a lot of time to act. But the picture isn't all bleak. There are success stories and individual beacons to point the way. One of these beacons is Peggy Shephard organizing her West Harlem community in New York City to neutralize the noxious impact of the nearby North River sewage treatment plant. "She took a groups of citizens who had lost faith in the system and convinced them that things can change."[5] Another beacon is Hazel Johnson performing a similar feat by bringing her Far Southside Chicago community together to fight its being used as a municipal toxic waste dump site after her husband had died from pollution induced lung cancer. "It's very difficult to get people to understand the importance of environment when they're struggling just to eat, to keep a roof over their heads and to educate their children, but Hazel has a way of organizing in her community."[6]

People like these are taking responsibility by engaging in, "antipolitical politics...(using) politics as one of the ways of seeking and achieving meaningful lives."[7] They are the newly powerful powerless who have risen to stand up for their beliefs and their existence in this often dehumanizing industrial age. Havel, in "The Power of the Powerless," characterizes the problem these potential beacons must overcome. "The crisis of contemporary technological society as a whole (is) the crisis that Heidegger describes as the ineptitude of humanity face to face with the planetary power of technology. Technology - that child of modern science...is out of humanity's control, has ceased to serve us, has enslaved us and compelled us to participate in the preparation of our own destruction. And humanity can find no way out: we have no idea and faith, and even less do we have a political conception to help us bring things back under human control."[8] But there are millions of incubating Peggy Shepards and Hazel Johnsons. One undeniable accomplishment of the American age is the encouragement of individual effort. Responsible individuals of conscience can direct their energies back into communities to make their cities habitable, their nations governable, and their civilization vital. "In other words, are not these informed non bureaucratic, dynamic, and open communities that comprise the 'parallel polis' a kind of rudimentary prefiguration, a symbolic model of those meaningful 'post-democratic' political structures that might become the foundation of a better society?"[9]

Thus, despairing First Worlders need not give up hope. There are paths to salvation. But reassessment, redirection, and reformation will not be easy. It cannot be done without massive individual involvement from the grass roots upward. It cannot be done by ceding power to bureaucracies and special interests. It cannot be done by 50 percent of the eligible voters. The personal and national resources are available. Does the collective will exist to develop this parallel polis, this politics of conscience? The answer to this single question more than any other will determine the fate of Western civilization.

THIRD WORLD VOICES FROM FIRST WORLD BODIES

As noted in Chapter 7, most industrial/technological nations have substantial contingents of Third Worlders in their midst. There are Africans in Western Europe, Hispanics in the United States, and Asians in Australia, groups which still contain many of the vital precepts that have withered in society at large. If family, community, tradition, and faith are to be rekindled in the First World these Third World enclaves may well be the catalyst, particularly as they become demographically more significant. They are where the real socio-political vitality rests in Western civilization. They are on the frontier of potential transformation. They are also the loci of the civilization's greatest challenges.

More than seventy years ago Frederick Jackson Turner analyzed the dynamism of the United States. "This perennial rebirth, this fluidity of American life, this expansion westward with its new opportunities, its continuous touch with the simplicity of primitive society, furnish the forces dominating the American character."[10] There are few, if any, geographic frontiers to conquer. However, demographic frontiers may uncover the basic principles, the vitality we seek. Those principles and structures which initially founded and framed Western civilization may hibernate within it today. Whether it be Native Americans in New Mexico, Vietnamese in New South Wales or Algerians in Provence, Third World voices are in position to reawaken their First World bodies, if permitted to do so. New governmental configurations and new societal actions may be required to facilitate this process.

In addition, to expanding the conscience and responsibility of individuals, there are other ways to configure and activate. Samuel Beer described one possibility[11]. The first presumption is that the United States, as the most complex but plastic industrial nation, will serve as proxy. A second presumption is that Third World enclaves, or other forces, are successful in igniting the resurgence of family, community, tradition, and faith. A third presumption is that Influence Spheres may present a new civilizational milieu. With those as a foundation Beer offers a description of a modification of Federalism that may serve to accommodate the pressures of our technological world.

The theory of small republics migrated from Machiavelli to Montesquieu and was refined by James Harrington. Its Seventeenth and Eighteenth Century manifestations were the United Netherland and the Swiss Cantons. The historical antecedent was the city states of ancient Greece. Early in our development as a nation this theory became a cornerstone tenet for the American Anti-Federalists. But it was less than optimally articulated and practiced under the Articles of Confederation of the 1780s. At that time it produced the mis-government that led to the Constitutional Convention of 1787. It may be the right time, in the coming Spherical World, for this theory to be explored once again. Large and pervasive government is not providing solutions. It is producing bureaucracies and gridlock plus removing the vital governing mechanisms farther and farther from the individual. If individual responsibility is to be encouraged, a method needs to be created for more effectively distributing power into the hands of those lives are impacted.

The small republic theory may provide a useful guideline. Central governments, even if they become supra-national, can focus their attention on matters of broad interest such as currency, foreign policy and defense. Aside from these functions their main responsibility will be to provide balancing or arbitration between various smaller constituencies. Beer sums up the reasons this concept can work as he restates the Anti-Federalist case: "The Anti-Federalist case is the 'argument from the community' which was latent in the existence of thirteen separate and long-settled colonies and which could find support not only in Montesquieu but also in some of the weightiest contributions to Western political thought going back to the Greeks. There was a high intellectual and moral appeal in their portraits of the civilizing effect of the common life of those close-knit bodies of people. In comparison with the extended republic, a polity of this sort could also be considered more democratic in the sense that its smaller area and greater homogeneity of interest made is closer to the people."[12]

Whether these smaller units would be villages, states, regions, cities, or even parts of cities would clearly depend on what is needed to fit the particular situation. Governmental constipation seems to require a halt to the expansion of central government authority and actually reverse the trend. By so doing the family and community can once again surface as organs of political responsibility, and energize reform. If First World nations are successful in effecting a regeneration of socio-political conscience and with it renewed civilizational vitality, a structure needs to develop which can give them a chance to breathe and to expand. The methodology for establishing and operating such a system within the United States is the subject of a forthcoming book.

We contend that a significant portion of the voices sounding chords of reason and stability inside industrial/technological entities emanate from Third World elements within and without. Responding to these voices with new governmental structures and new bundles of principles may be the only way to keep Western civilization from spinning drastically out of control.

SUBSISTENCE

That the current pervasiveness of nuclear weapons could cause a disaster in the course of some military action is becoming an increasing likelihood. So many nations have access to this terrible technology that it may be unreasonable to assume continued universal restraint. Hopefully, the use of nuclear weapons or their cheaper but equally as dangerous compatriots in the chemical and biological category, will be confined to tactical rather than strategic employment. Whether they are or not, some sort of regional, if not apocalyptic, nuclear destruction appears to loom on the horizon, possibly emanating from the expected warfare in the Middle East.

In addition widespread settlement of peoples in disregard of natural phenomenon such as earthquakes, floods, and drought has made them more vulnerable to large scale disaster. With populations of disadvantaged escalating and financial resources stretched thin everywhere the number of rootless and destitute is likely to escalate as the next century gets underway. Their societal structures will have been decimated.

The multitudes now pouring into cities, particularly in the Third World, are very exposed to the spread of pestilence, despite advances in medical technology. Even today many Third World cities, not to mention First World ghettos, are places where malnutrition, sickness, high infant mortality, and short life spans run rampant. This condition promises to become worse as urban areas expand.

Thus, by the middle of the next century a substantial portion of the world may have to reconstitute itself after undergoing some level of destruction. The first step will be establishment of a subsistence society. Subsistence living could cover more of the earth than it does now and that we are currently prepared to acknowledge. As people struggle to survive they will begin to rebuild societies from the bottom up. As in all such primal groupings the basic pillars of family, community faith, and tradition will loom very large by necessity. Therefore the most vital civilizational components may emerge from the areas that have undergone the greatest privation. As these societies move through the subsistence level they could become cradles of incipient civilizations.

---

[1] As quoted by Archibald Cox in the *Harvard Alumni Gazette* March, 1992.

[2] Fernand Braudel, "Civilization and Capitalism 15th -18th Century - Vol. 3," *The Perspective of the World*, trans. Sián Reynolds (Harper Collins, 1984) p. 85.

[3] Christopher Lasch, *The True and Only Heaven - Progress and Its Critics* (W.W. Norton & Co., NY, 1991) p. 532.

[4] Václav Havel "Politics and Conscience", *Open Letters*, ed. by Paul Wilson (Vintage Books, NY, 1991) p. 263.

5 Michael Lipske, "People Who Make a Difference," *National Wildlife*, Oct.-Nov., 1993, pp 45-46.
6 Ibid., pp 50-51.
7 Václav Havel, "Politics and Conscience" *Open Letters*, ed. by Paul Wilson (Vintage Books, NY, 1991) p.269
8 Václav Havel, "Power of the Powerless" *Open Letters*, ed. by Paul Wilson (Vintage Books, NY, 1991) p. 206
9 Václav Havel, "Power of the Powerless" *Open Letters*, ed. by Paul Wilson (Vintage Books, NY, 1991) p.213.
10 Frederick Jackson Turner, *The Frontier in American History* (New York, 1921) p. 3.
11 Samuel Beer, *To Make a Nation: The Rediscovery of American Federalism* (The Belknap Press of Harvard University Press, Cambridge, MA , 1993) pp 219-278.
12 Ibid., pp 242-243.

CHAPTER 12

Post-Technological Polity

The preposition 'post' means after. It implies sequence, not disappearance. The world of the Twenty-First Century will not be required to exist without technology, but probably in an environment which it doesn't dominate. Therefore, the difference will be the role for, not necessarily the nature of, technology.

The position of technology in today's world seems analogous to that of Alexandria's Mouseion, its repository of scientific knowledge, to the Third Century B.C. E.M. Forster described the situation. "It did not bring happiness or wisdom: science never does. But it explored the physical universe and harnessed many powers for our use."[1] If we are to properly harness these powers, it is time for the First World to take the next step. Values need to be brought into perspective. Technology must become one of society's pistons and not remain the entire engine. This is not an unremittingly anti-technological position. There have been great benefits received. But increasingly technological development has become societally counter-productive. More frighteningly the technological methods for operating an Orwellian autocracy are readily available and could be implemented even with ostensibly good intentions. We desperately need to rearrange our priorities to restore basic principles to their rightful position at the foundation of Western civilization. The restructuring process can take several forms. Some of these could provide for the continued viability of the

American age. All will create room for the rise of new civilizational entities.

THE SCOPE OF THE INFLUENCE SPHERES

As already noted, Influence Spheres are currently forming centered upon the United States, Japan, and Germany. The rates of formation, the consistency of coagulation, the relation to contiguous areas all depend upon a host of variables. We can imagine each sphere, "as an integrated whole, within which each society functions like a slowly spinning top, its gyrations keeping time with ecological and social processes."[2] The speed, the degree of wobble, the duration of spin all react to different stimuli. So will the spheres themselves. For simplicity's sake only two of the possible paths these entities could assume will be inspected. They bracket the others.

Optimistic assumptions (from the vantage point of the First World) envision a prolongation of Western civilization's prominence through a relatively smooth transition from nation-state to regional leader for each of these spherical centers. This could occur if regional amalgamations coincide with a restoration of basic precepts. In the United States, for example, this process, "will call for new generations of Americans who have grown up in nurturing family, school, and community environments and will have learned since early childhood the value of personal empowerment."[3] Such a process, while not impossible, would require a significant redirection of national resources plus a concentration of collective focus.

This evolution would presume the development of a strong sense of duty supplementing established individualism. It would also necessitate creation of a national sense of balance between individual power, individual obligations, and mutual appreciation of abilities. "Clearly, liberty and excellence are powerfully related, It is not, of course, true, conversely, that equality and mediocrity need to go together. It is entirely possible to think of a political community of outstanding equals. Such a community would seem to be a contradiction in terms. because to be outstanding is precisely not to be equal. Yet such a community is thinkable. If all members stand out in their particular way, we could have something like a forest of unusually well grown and various trees - all excellent in growth and all piercing the sky to about the same height."[4] Does this sound fanciful or unattainably utopian? It may appear that way because such a society would be very difficult to achieve, but Václav Havel's ideals (among others) encompass such a community.

If democracy, free markets, and individuality all hallmarks of the American age of Western civilization, are to comfortably co-exist, something almost utopian will have to emerge. While bigger and more authoritarian government might be deemed necessary to confront complex problems, it would be prone to tread on freedoms and individuality. Thus it would be a definitive step in another direction. Wealth accumulation or personal freedoms could be subjected to the forced curtailments of leveling and redistribution, but this too would herald a different direction. There is only one logical method if this country wishes to produce individuals of responsibility and of conscience who can mold effective government out of our disparate demographic groups, while facing the world's sophisticated challenges and remaining within the democratic-republican tradition of the United States. It must strive for a society of unusually well grown and various trees in a community of outstanding equals. Anything less would be a violation of the aspirations of the American age. Anything other than reinforcement of the basic pillars of family, community, tradition,and faith would be an abandonment of Havel's ideals. This combination is necessarily delicate, but not impossible.

Accomplishing this in a First World society, such as the United States, would involve an intricate series of steps. These would lead us in a slight retreat from reliance on technology and from pondering individuality while substituting an advance in communal reinforcement and familial self-sufficiency. Governmental power might need to be distributed into smaller configurations. The definitions of extended families and communities would need to be expanded to permit them to supplement socio-economic institutions. Faith would have to be restored to a meaningful place in everyday lives. Perhaps there is a combination that would serve this purpose. As previously mentioned, an adaptation of Montesquieu's small republic theory blended with Václav Havel's politics of conscience is one such combination. There may be others. We need to explore them all. We must somehow preserve individual freedoms by impregnating them with a sense of individual responsibility and thereby broaden available opportunities. The result could prolong the life of Western civilization.

The most likely site for this to occur would be in an Influence Sphere based upon the United States. The principles are the freshest, the resources most abundant, the distractions least bothersome. It could begin as a North American confederation, in many ways similar to NAFTA. In time it could expand to include additional areas of Central and South America. A Central European version of this confederation based upon a German speaking spine is also possible. It could fill out to include both Western and Eastern adjuncts in a larger Influence Sphere.

This constitutes the optimistic case. Many changes need to take place for it to happen - in individual attitudes, in political structure, in economic practice. While its pure form remains the best hope for Western civilization, in modified form a development of this type could create the likelihood of relative socio-political calm. Without at least some movement toward such a blend the American age of Western civilization appears to be embarked upon a perilous journey.

The Pessimistic case involves fragmentation. There are ethnic, social, and economic pressures upon most industrial/technological nations. If not properly attended they could create internal strife and eventual dismemberment. The financial and sociological resources available to combat the various challenges are limited, unless major life-style revisions are effected. Imbedded poverty, demographic conflict, aging work forces, and gridlocked governments compound the problems. Without individual attitudinal revisions and lengthening political horizons the nations at the center of the industrial/technological age could be poised on the brink of implosion or atomization.

It may not be that the actual scenario will turn out to be as disastrous as this implication of civil strife and economic collapse. But even its partial enactment would rob Western civilization of its momentum. This is well within the realm of possibility. It seems almost incontrovertible that the eclipse of this civilization's world domination is underway. What is at issue is how viable its legatees, the resultant Influence-Spheres, will become. Their individual vitality will determine the perseverance of the American age, the degree of its transformation, and the scope of its remaining influence. Spheres of some sort centered on the United States and Germany seem likely to flourish well into the Twenty-First Century. How far, how extensive, how vibrant will depend on how rapidly and effectively internal problems are handled and inclusive mechanisms are developed. At the moment the probabilities are no better than even for any Influence Sphere to remain a cohesive influential entity past the first half of the next century.

BUDDING THEOCRACY

Two conditions are likely to characterize the process of forming civilizations: strong religious convictions and violence. Both emanate from the desperation of deprivation and the yearning for recognition as equal human beings.

Studs Terkel, while conducting interviews for his book. "Race", uncovered a succinct articulation of why people with little to lose often turn to violence. "You know how poverty breeds a terrible savagery. It eliminates so many of the conscious things that control your behavior."[5] It can be difficult for people who are earnestly attempting to effect improvements form their seats amid privilege and power to understand violent actions. It can be difficult for them to identify with people whose prospects seem so unequivocally bleak and who therefore possess very different personal risk/reward ratios.

While the fact that committed fanatics are only a small minority in most societies, they are frightening for the example they set. The real threat to the world's equilibrium is its growing multitudes of poor, especially urban poor. The more hopeless these people believe their relative condition to be the more they are susceptible to those who preach violence as a solution. The less they value their own lives, the less they will value the lives of others. Savagery is an instant equalizer, both physically and psychologically. Alas, every day more of the disadvantaged are turning to it.

Another equalizer throughout history has been religion. Despite its frequent hierarchical and authoritarian structure, it promises equality to all - in the eyes of the Almighty. The laser-like purity and simplicity of this promise is galvanizing. A religious quest for equality has been at the eye of most civilization formations and could constitute an attractive alternative to the materialism of the American age. Kenneth Clark capsulized this eternal challenge when discussing St. Francis of Assisi. "His belief that in order to free the spirit we must shed our earthly goods is the belief that all great religious teachers have had in common - Eastern and Western without exception."[6] The simple egalitarian thrust of fundamentalism, in most of its guises, advertises this tenet forthrightly and is as much a threat to the industrial nations at the heart of the American age as the followers of St. Francis were to the Thirteenth Century Catholic church. One of the reasons that the Inquisition was established was to crush this trend of belief which was labeled a heresy.

Fundamentalism in its various expressions offers several other features that are proving attractive to an increasing number of people, not merely the disadvantaged. It closes the gap between church and state, bringing religion into all aspects of daily life and government. It offers a rigid code of behavior usually through literal textural interpretation. Thus, for fundamentalists there is little ambiguity over how they should act in any given situation. Their code normally is very traditional. It obviates what they believe to be the confusions and corruptions of modern practices. Finally, fundamentalists have restored a sense of mystery to their lives through Messianic concepts. In a world where technology reigns, even to the attempted quantification of God, this combination of ordering and mystifying can be seductively attractive.

As they have in centuries past, the new civilizations of the future will obtain much of their initial power from the violent desperation of poverty, the desire for equality, and the yearning for structure. The main targets of these gathering forces will be the proprietors of enslaving technology and perceived decadence who are personified by the bastions of power and elitism governing the prime movers of the American age. The engines of dissemination will be fundamentalist religions.

ISLAMIC VIBRATIONS

Islam is rapidly becoming the religion of choice for many of the world's disadvantage. Its manifestations can be separated into five ethno-geographic categories, each with different practices and prospects.

First of all there are the Arabs. Most of these are Sunni. Most live in poverty in the Middle East, in close proximity to vast reserves of oil. Most are currently ruled by Western-oriented or Western-dependent elites. Their habitation extends along the North African Mediterranean littoral and into the northern portions of the Sudan. It encompasses the Arabian Peninsula and reaches in a broad band up through Iraq, Jordan, Lebanon, and Syria. The holiest Islamic sites are contained in the Saudi Arabian cities of Mecca and Medina. The Arabic nations are the seat both of the religion's origins and of its deepest cultural traditions. For these reasons Arabs, while only loosely connected, in many ways collectively consider themselves first among Muslims.

Turkic peoples inhabit most of Turkey, some of Azeribaijan, and make up most of the population of the Central Asian republics of the former Soviet Union. Some of the Muslims in Afghanistan and Pakistan are ethnically similar. Turkic peoples comprised the spearheads of the most virulent Islamic invasions from Central Asia into the Indian Peninsula, the Middle East, and Europe. They also established the most powerful and persistent Islamic empire - the Ottoman.

The bulk of the Shi'ite population is located in Iran, Southern Iraq and Azeribaijan. They have political and religious links with Algeria, the Sudan, and Egypt. Throughout Islamic history clerics have been most closely and fiercely connected to government in Shi'ite nations. The same is true today.

Southeast Asia harbors large populations of Muslims in Bangladesh, Malaysia, and Indonesia. Most are Sunni with traditions linking them to India's Mughul Empire.

Finally, there are the Muslims of the Diaspora. Originally they were virtually all immigrants with ties to their native lands. Increasingly they are indigenous with agendas of their own.

Fundamentalism enjoys increasing acceptance within Islamic nations, and has taken on increasingly upsetting (for Western or Western-oriented powers) connotations outside them. Religious, or near-religious states, currently exist in Iran, Sudan, Algeria, and Afghanistan. Egypt is teetering. The Sunni Wahabi conservatism of Saudi Arabia is getting more involved in the functions of government. In the West, Fundamental Islam produces images of the Ayatollah Khomeni waving the Koran before millions of adoring fanatics. It conjures up nightmares of terrorism, anti-Western diatribes, hostages, and implacable hostility to material, technological lifestyles. Unfortunately, these images are increasingly becoming reality largely due to the West's overreaction to fundamentalist rhetoric and its indifference to the needs of the Muslim disadvantaged. The masses of uncommitted Muslims, looking mainly for a better life, are gradually being pushed into the camp of the fundamental activists who are seen by them as being most able to prize forth concessions.

Before the next century is too far along there is likely to be some resurrection of an Arab civilization under fundamentalist aegis. This vision could produce a degree of unity among the Arab masses not presently envisaged as possible. It will be less important whether it is nominally Sunni or Shiite led than whether it contains the basic fundamentalist traits of a militant religious society. At least in the early years these traits will be necessary in order to provide the cohesion and purpose required to energize largely disadvantaged and habitually impotent populations and gain control of the vital oil fields. Eventually, fundamentalism will fade as it has in the past and fissures in the ephemeral Arab unity will once again appear. This unity, however briefly enjoyed, could for a time surmount the religious, political, and ethnic differences which have always promoted fragmentation, and create an incendiary force.

Looked at from the vantage point of the multitude of Arab poor, who are almost never seen or heard, there is great yearning for charismatic leadership that promises to recapture a patrimony of economic, cultural, and religious assets from the West and its minions. Although Nasser, Sadat,and Saddam were all secular leaders, the most likely source for such charisma is the latent energy of the Koran. Under its religious banner an Arab force could sweep the area sometime early in the Twenty-First Century, gathering the oil fields into its folds. This unity may last for the blink of an historical eyelash and is not likely to take place without some sort of Sunni-Shi'ite conflict, but when it materializes it could be temporarily comprehensive and destructive to Western interests.

The Turkic peoples that are scattered from the Bosphorous to the Taklamakan Desert are already beginning to cooperate. They border on strategic, but fluid and volatile, areas in the Caucasus, the Middle East, the Southern flank of Russia, the Indian Peninsula, and China. Some of their homelands contain rich mineral resources. They lie astride ancient transportation routes. They have histories rich in conquest and splendor. They are bookended by two nations, Turkey and Pakistan, with a Western orientation that has provided some economic and military might.

The forces of unity in these areas are likely to be less fundamentally religious than they are economic and ethnic. An escalating turmoil on all sides, in which they may wish to be only peripherally and intermittently involved, could weld them closer together.

While this union could be less intense and slower to develop than that of the Arabs, it is likely to last longer. The eventual forms of government, be it autocracy or democracy, secular or religious, confederation or alliance, will depend largely upon the nature of outside pressure and assistance.

The Muslims of Bangladesh, Malaysia, and Indonesia are likely to be so caught up in the conflicts of East and Southeast Asia that they will have little chance to unite or even seek common ground. The resources and productivity of Malaysia and Indonesia could well become targets of the tides of conquest washing over the area. Other Muslim peoples (as well as non-Muslims) caught along the fault lines of forming civilizations or confederations, could find themselves crushed. The Kurds are a good example of a people exposed to this risk.

The world's one billion Muslims are reproducing at a faster rate than its population as a whole. By the next century they should account for the largest demographic body covered by a single religion. Situated and endowed as they are, Islamic people will play a major role in determining the development and configuration of the Twenty-First Century world, despite their inherent differences.

There are two potential civilizations for the next century based upon Islam. Should they develop, both would be firmly grounded in the principles of family, community, faith, and tradition so necessary for any vital civilization. However, the intensity of their faith could differ dramatically. One difference would constitute a religiously oriented revival of Arab culture and the other would be a more secular combination of Turkic states.

CHRISTIAN FUNDAMENTALS

There are two forms of Christian fundamentalism now being energized in North and South America. They have different demographic bases and, thus, separate goals. But together they are likely to provide the strongest unifying force in the Americas and a prime source of any civilizational revival.

In the United States the 'religious right' is identified with elements of the Southern Baptist Convention, The Christian Coalition, and Christian Reconstructionism, among others. These believers all advocate strict, often literal, adherence to the words of the Bible. They are normally traditionalists who favor small central government, capitalistic economies, and who live largely in the suburbs (which now account for 51% of the United States' population). They want to protect their lives from the inroads of what is seen as rampant licentiousness - represented by pornography, rap music, babies out of wedlock, drugs, and the inner city poor. They fight to preserve their 'American Dream' which is squarely founded upon those familiar four pillars of family, community, faith, and tradition. Conservative religious forces are becoming an increasing power in United States' politics, education, and social thinking. They may polarize, they may subvert, they may frighten but they cannot be ignored. More significantly, they represent an attractive life style alternative for an increasing number of citizens battered by the rootlessness of modern industrial/technological society.

In Latin America Evangelical Protestants, mostly Pentacostal Christians, now comprise almost ten percent of the region's 450 million people with major representations in Brazil, Chile, Peru, El Salvador, and Guatemala. They have co-opted religious momentum from the Catholic Church. Their services, which are conducted in Spanish, supply those miraculous, mysterious, charismatic interpretations of the New Testament those anxious for a more relevant religion felt were lacking. Although Latin evangelicals are inspired by United States mother churches and their missionaries, they comprise a different class of people with a different purpose than Protestant fundamentalists in the home country.

In Latin America it is generally the Hispanic urban poor (as differentiated from the poor Indians whose native beliefs surface as thinly disguised Catholicism) who make up the congregations. They are energized by the possibilities opened up to them through evangelicalism. These include self-improvement, upward mobility, and monetary gain through capitalistic entrepreneurship. It is these people, from the slums of the sprouting metropoli, who most need rescue. Turning them into possible bastions of democracy and free markets would immeasurably enhance Latin American prospects and bind their people closer to Northern Hispanics. Already Pentacostal Christians have played major roles in Guatemalan, Peruvian, and Chilean elections. They have also become a significant economic factor in Brazil. Combining their basic tendencies, toward family and community with a reinvigorated spiritual life and new politico-economic principles, could extend both the life and the grasp of the American age in ways that currently seem frightening to many who are wedded to traditional societal forms.

Some people are put off by the prospect of religious fundamentalism with its enforced structures and expressed intolerance. There is no question that in many ways the life the fundamentalists seek in the United States would be less indulgent, less sybaritic and in some ways possibly less pleasant than that enjoyed by the middle and upper classes. It is evident fulfillment is proving elusive when there is a yearning in so many for 'something more in life'. The absence of a generally accepted ethical value structure is creating a gap in many lives. Fundamental religion is proving a moral panacea for those desperately in need of it. In both Latin America and the United States Protestant Christian fundamentalists combined with Hispanic communities could help rediscover the path toward a greater sense of morality and ethics in political, economic, and social activities and in the process produce more widespread economic benefits. If families and communities are to revive and assume responsibilities, it may require a core of fundamental believers to act as a catalyst. Such individuals are becoming involved in the system, in both North and South America. Their example may create a more positive and vigorous climate for the organization and revitalization of society. However, the deprecatory, exclusionary aspects of their beliefs need to be tempered if this influence is to be positive.

In this way a new form of Western civilization could develop in the Americas. It could be a neo-American age. The ingredients are present. Possibly fundamental Christian movements can help make them gel. A unified, economically vibrant, socially progressive United States and Latin America together could have a significant world presence lasting throughout the next century. To realize this favorable outcome all the Americas, particularly the United States as their flywheel, would have to restructure politically, develop financial sanity, bring life styles in line with resources, avoid demographic mine fields, and begin immediately to strengthen the pillars of their civilization. This will not be easy. At least the possibility for revival exists. No other industrial/technological Influence Sphere can make as optimistic an assertion.

THE EAST ASIAN VOLCANO

The contest for control of the territory and the resources of East Asia among the area's burgeoning martial entities is likely to consume much, if not all, of the Twenty-First Century's initial half. The major combatants will be China and India whose three billion inhabitants could comprise almost forty percent of the world's population by 2025. The contest will most likely involve warfare.

In analyzing how a military action could develop, it is worth noting what Scott Boorman pointed out in his prescient book *The Protracted Game*[7]. East Asian military commanders have two sources for their strategic philosophies. Those who are Western-oriented have a confrontational enemy-destroying tradition based upon chess. Boorman carefully annotated the Oriental traditions accumulated over the centuries by playing Wei'chi (or Go). This very different strategy employs surrounding or area-controlling techniques. The Vietnam War was an excellent illustration of what happens when one meets the other. As the military situation develops the chess-oriented, Western nations (India, Russia, North and South Korea, possibly Thailand) versus the Go-oriented, Eastern ones China, Vietnam, Japan) influences will be vie for supremacy. This will happen both within coalitions and between combatants. Philosophy, as well as armaments, will affect how armies are commanded and how war is waged. One thing seems certain. The coming collision, particularly the desire to control territory, will create many casualties and much hardship among the civilian population. Warfare in East Asia will not be 'clean' and is likely to involve wide swaths of destruction, millions of dead and wounded, and nuclear weapons, probably of a tactical nature.

East Asia is rapidly becoming the most heavily armed sector of the world. It has many pockets of growing prosperity. It also has potentially exposed industrial centers like Singapore, Hong Kong,

Penang, and Bangkok. It has long supply and production routes open to interdiction. Japan is a prime illustration. As has been historically the case, the home islands have a shortage of raw materials and arable land relative to their population, necessitating importation of resources and products. These rely on far-flung sources of supply and are hard to defend. Distances in the Pacific and in East Asia are immense. This region is normally not self-sufficient in food. India will have even less arable land per capita in the future as its population expands. China contains one quarter of the world's people on seven percent of its arable land. East Asia has ancient cultures with an equally ancient history of conflict. In short, the area is a tinder box, heavily armed, short of space and resources, amply supplied with resentments, and dominated by economic elites. It is extremely difficult to prognosticate what alliances might form, where battles might be fought and what civilizations might emerge. However, there are probabilities which can be identified. Japan is the primary East Asian economic power today. The People's Republic of China is being touted as the power of the future. The four tigers: Singapore, Taiwan, Hong Kong, and South Korea are recent economic miracles. The area as a whole has the highest real economic growth rate of any region in the world.

Due to a combination of rapidly changing internal socio-economics and external vulnerabilities, Japan's power may be on the wane. It may have to form a series of alliances to assure its own viability. Russia would be a logical partner whose assets (natural resources, military forces) and needs (money, technology) match up well against Japan. Once the Kurile Islands question is settled this partnership would be ready to commence. Between them lies a divided Korea, historically stretched by forces from Japan, China, and Russia. Korea's economic resources and military prowess could be an important adjunct to any partnership, but its adherence is likely to be dominated by the disposition of North China.

Southeast Asia has always been an important source of agricultural and industrial resources to Japan, China ,and India alternating intermittently. While its agriculture remains significant, it is as an industrial manufacturing center, particularly for Japan, that its current importance is based. Its allegiance will be actively sought. Invasions are probable by those who feel threatened or disappointed.

China's economic and military potential is enormous, as has been pointed out by countless observers. Its biggest problem, apart from periodic incursions from without, has been a chronic inability to keep its nation unified. Prosperity in the South and militarism in the North have repeatedly been in opposition. This age old dichotomy is expected to resurface before China can reach its eventual potential. At least one, possibly temporary, separation is expected. If China is to initiate any major warfare, it is more likely to result from interference and seepage across sensitive borders, particularly in the South and Southwest, than from large scale invasion. Conversely, if an attack is received it is likely to be massive.

India is bursting at its seams, its population is exploding and it is riven by internal strife. Hemmed in on three sides by the sea and channeled by Muslim nations on its Northeast and Northwest frontiers, one axis of eruption points directly towards Tibet and Western China. It also has traditions in Southeast Asia and a hunger for its assets. It has a potentially powerful military-industrial base. A mission of conquest could stave off disintegration, unify its people, and offer solutions to its future deficits. Warlike activities are prominent in its past. Militant Hinduism is once again reviving, spreading, and bumping up against more pacific elements. India could be the initiator of an East Asian conflict as it seeks room for growth. One motive could be the opportunity to pry loose Southeastern China by backing its independence. Another could be territorial gain to the north, or assets to the east.

There are likely to be many clashes of all sizes, involving many countries in changing combinations. Nevertheless, it is hard to disregard the likelihood of a basic North-South confrontation with allies ranging themselves along geographic lines. That would put India at the center of the Southern coalition, strongly buttressed economically by Southern China, looking for respite from enviously repressive regulation and militarily by Vietnam, looking once again to revive its prospects by establishing an empire. A key variable will be the ability of the Philippines, Malaysia, Indonesia, and Australia to remain disengaged and uninvaded. A Northern group would include Japan, East Russia (possibly split from a weakening center), North China, and the Koreas. The main battlefields of such a collision would be in both Southwest and West-Central China as well as in Southeast Asia, where Japanese interests would meet the Chinese Navy.

Of course any scenario is merely conjecture. But the likelihood of some major clash in the area seems high. The current status of the several military establishments indicate that high technology will not be a main feature. Infantry will be by far the most prevalent fighting force. Air support of ground forces would be minimal, although some tactical air power could be employed.

Strategic air will be supplied mostly by missiles, of which Japan has a particularly sophisticated knowledge. There is likely to be some naval activity as, for the first time since Kublai Khan, China is building a blue water navy, capable of controlling the South China Sea into the Indian Ocean. Lightly sprinkled throughout all these forces will be a few examples of highly sophisticated weaponry. Most of these will be in the area of missile defense systems and guidance control. The end result of all of this activity would be to divert economic growth and development in East Asia from their anticipated paths until the latter half of the Twenty-First Century.

If military conflict should take place as outlined several important questions will have to be answered. Can the West stay out? If not, where will it place its support? What will happen to the massive economic investments? Will they be converted to military use? What role will the Pakistanis and the Central Asian Muslims play?

These questions prompt thoughts if not answers. The West, battered by intervention attempts in the early 1990s, and preoccupied with internal problems, will not be prone to involvement. Its major concern will be economic - the loss of investments, production, and markets. Investments and other vested interests have not stopped previous wars, but piecemeal attempts to address these concerns, plus pure greed, might encourage Western nations to supply arms, technology, and possibly some specialized troops to both sides. On the other hand, its two Influence Spheres could benefit by profitably remaining on the periphery of the storm.

There are many who believe economic growth and rising standards of living will restrain East Asia from engaging in warfare. Perhaps this is the case. Europe never allowed those conditions to deter them.

There is no doubt that should these events take place as depicted they will constitute World War III. The Twentieth Century, it must be remembered, withstood two world wars. The First, being largely regional, will be the one the East Asian conflict will most likely resemble. After each World War the damage was repaired, the map was redrawn and new heights of achievements awaited.

In previous periods of over-population and over use of the environment the penalties exacted by disease, natural disasters, and warfare has been between one-quarter and one-third of an area's inhabitants. That seems to be a realistic damage figure for East and Central Asia should the proposed conflicts unfold.

Some of the societies in the afflicted regions will have to be rebuilt from the ground up. Others will have to undergo major reconstruction. Throughout history wars have never acted as a bar to civilizational growth. On the contrary, they have often fostered it. That is likely to happen again. There are two civilizations that could develop. In the South a civilization of Indian outreach and cultural influence is possible. This occurred several times in the years between the Second and the Sixteenth Centuries. However, its pulse and cohesion have always been, and are likely to be, relatively weak. In the North the thriving civilizational force has usually been Chinese (often with Mongolian or Manchurian infusions). This is likely to recur, characterized by traditional North Chinese austerity, organization, and energy. Japan will, as usual, retain some detachment, and will probably be an adjunct in any combination. As it has been repeatedly, Siberia will be a potential prize. Russia will be torn between protecting it and dealing with other disruptions across its vastness. Siberia may well detach itself.

Any North-South contest seems likely to be won by the North. Eventually China should be reunited under Northern domination to resume its delayed destiny. In this way China could finally achieve its economic and cultural potential, possibly augmented by a level of world power not seen since Genghis Khan.

Could this be all wrong? Could Asia be headed for a century of peace and prosperity based upon economic dynamism and political stability? Absolutely. In fact this is more or less the substance of most predictions by current pundits. The differing outlook stated herein assumes that military conflict in East Asia is inevitable, with the only unknown being the degree of intensity.

CONVERGING PATHS AND EMERGING VALUES

The Second World has evaporated. The First and Third appear headed for a period where they progressively grow closer together. This will be partially due to economic growth in some previously underdeveloped areas. It will be partially due to life style reductions in developed areas resulting from financial and other resource limitations.

Christopher Lasch put his finger on the attitude that reflects these limitations and that ultimately will bring the two into greater conformity intellectually, emotionally, and physically. "While modern industry condemns people to jobs that insult their intelligence, the mass culture of romantic escape fills their heads with visions of experience beyond their means - beyond their emotional and imaginative capacities as well - and this contributes to a further devaluation of routine...cripples the will to change social conditions, to make even modest improvements in work and play, and to restore meaning and dignity to everyday life."[8]

The Third World is already providing inspiration for the re-establishment of basic values. It is illustrating how to combine imagination and meaning through religion. It displays examples of dignity through tradition. Above all, it is striving to show how to overcome dehumanizing routine through family and community. The First World is floundering emotionally and materially. It is seeking guideposts to return it to the track.

World realignment is as necessary now as it has been at numerous critical junctures of history. The process, as ever, will be arduous and uneven. In Europe the Eleventh Century turmoil set the stage for the process of the flowering of the Twelfth and the Thirteenth Centuries. In China tribulations in the late Fifth and early Sixth Centuries preceded the Tang magnificence. In Meso-America the Seventh Century disruption was herald to the greatest of the Maya Classic age. We do know that the world is entering a period of unusual challenge and uncertainty. At this particular juncture the less developed societies may have more to offer future civilization than their more materially advantaged compatriots. This is positive for the longer term. It is yet unclear how willing to learn, how self-motivated the First World will be in reforming. We still do not know how much will have to be forced upon it by crisis. It is not decided whether the East Asians will temper opportunity with judgment. Maybe they can sustain prosperity without serious conflict. Maybe they will emulate the Europeans of 1914. The answers to these questions will determine both the depth of incipient turmoil and the height of forthcoming accomplishments.

Looking back over the events of the Twentieth Century any historian would observe much violence, conflict, and unrest. There were also unprecedented advances. The coming century is not likely to be any less violent and turbulent. Its achievements will be no less spectacular. All will be different. They will involve different areas of the world. They will employ different desires and different concepts. Prognosticators peering forward through the mists of time need not to entertain a greater degree of pessimism than did their predecessors of the 1890s. They need not water down their ideals any more than was done one hundred years ago. Most importantly, those looking into the future must heed a primary lesson of history and not be afraid of change, either of axis or of amplitude.

---

1 E.M. Forster, *Alexandria, Illustrated History and Guide* (Peter Smith)

2 Jay Miller, "A Kinship of Spirit," *America in 1492*, ed. Alvin Joseph, (Alfred A. Knopf, NY, 1992) p. 309.

3 James MacGregor Burns and Stewart Burns, *A People's Charter* (Alfred A. Knopf, NY, 1991) p. 466.

4 Eva T. H. Brann, dean of St. John's College, Annapolis, MD in an address, "Democratic Distinction" delivered to initiates of the George Washington University Chapter of Phi Beta Kappa on May 8, 1993.

5 Studs Terkel, *Race,* interview with Ed Reardon (New Press, NY, 1992) p. 268.

6 Kenneth Clark, *Civilization* (Harper Perennial Books, NY, 1969) p. 78.

7 *The Protracted Game* (Oxford University Press, 1969).

8 Christopher Lasch, *The Culture of Narcissism* (W.W. Norton & Company, NY, 1976) p. 96.

Afterword

Plotinus, "turned aside from the spectacle of ruin and misery in the actual world, to contemplate an eternal world of goodness and beauty."[1] In this book I have attempted to employ reason and not emotion to confront often unpleasant realities in a search for solutions and solace.

I have tried to point out choices as well as probabilities. I have also immersed any traumas in the sweep of history intending to provide perspective.

Machiavelli wrote in his *Discourses*, almost one hundred years ago, "no great events ever occur in any city or country that have not been predicted by soothsayers, revelations, or by portents."[2] Whether or not I qualify as a soothsayer, I have striven to discover revelations and portents lodged in the worldscape before us.

I have been encouraged in my writing by the words of John Stuart Mill. "Truth gains more by the errors of one who, with due study and preparation, thinks for himself, than by the true opinions of those who only hold them because they do not suffer themselves to think."[3] Right or wrong the opinions are my own. My hope is that their value will lie beyond mere validity by igniting a debate which may develop alternative approaches to our civilization's problems and opportunities.

CSG
Cotuit, November, 1993

---

1 Bertrand Russell, *A History of Western Philosophy* (Simon & Schuster, NY, 1945) p. 284.

2 Machiavelli, *Discourses*, Book One, chapter fifty-five

3 John Stuart Mill, *Utilitarianism, Liberty, and Representative Government* (Everyman Library, New York, 1950) p. 125-6.

Bibliography

Allen, William Francis. *A Short History of the Roman Empire.* Boston, 1890.

Alperovitz, Gar. "The Economic Summit Won't Matter," *New York Times*, (16 December 1992).

Andrews, Charles Maclean. "These Forty Years," *American Historical Review* 30. (January 1925).

Bailyn, Bernard. *The Debate on the Constitution - Federalist and Antifederalist Speeches, Articles, and Letters During the Struggle Over Ratification.* New York: Library of America, 1993.

Barker, Sir Ernest, ed. *Social Contract - Essays by Locke, Hume, and Rousseau.* Oxford: Oxford University Press, 1947.

Bancroft, George. "The Office of the People in Art, Government, and Religion," *Literary and Historical Miscellanies.* New York, 1885.

Barraclough, Geoffrey. *Introduction to Contemporary History.* Middlesex: Pelican Books, 1967.

-------. "The Great World Crisis I," *New York Review of Books*, (23 January 1975).

-------. "Wealth and Power: The Politics of Food and Oil," *New York Review of Books*, (7 August 1975).

-------. "Planning for a New Economic Order," *New York Review of Books*, (16 August 1975).

-------. "The Haves and the Have Nots," *New York Review of Books*, (13 May 1976).

-------. "Waiting for a New World Order," *New York Review of Books,* 26 October 1978.

-------. "The Struggle for the Third World," *New York Review of Books*, (9 November 1978).

Beer, Samuel H. *To Make a Nation - The Rediscovery of American Federalism.* Cambridge: The Belknap Press of Harvard University Press, 1993.

Bloch, Marc. *The Historian's Craft.* New York: Random House, 1953.

Brann, Eva T.H. "Democratic Distinction," *The Key Reporter* 58, no. 4 (Summer 1993). address to the initiates of George Washington University Phi Beta Kappa Chapter.

Braudel, Fernand. *The Mediterranean and the Mediterranean World in the Age of Philip II.* New York: Harper Colophon Books, 1972.

-------. *Civilization and Capitalism 15th - 18th Century.* New York: Harper & Row, 1982.

-------. *A History of Civilizations.* New York: Allen Lane, The Penguin Press, 1994.

Brzezinski, Zbignew. *Out of Control - Global Turmoil on the Eve of the 21st Century.* New York: Charles Scribners and Sons, 1993.

-------. *The Fragile Blossom.* New York: Harper & Row, 1972.

Brown, William G. *The Life of Oliver Ellsworth.* New York, 1905. Irvine, CA: Reprint Services, Notable American Authors, 1991.

Bryce, Lord James. *The American Commonwealth.* 1888.

Burgess, John William. "The Methods of Historical Study and Research in Columbia College," in *Methods of Teaching and Studying History.* Edited by Stanley G. Hall. Boston, 1886.

-------. *The Foundations of American Political Science.* New York, 1933.

Burns, MacGregor James. *The Vineyard of Liberty.* New York: Alfred A. Knopf, 1982.

------., and Burns Stuart. *A People's Charter: The Pursuit of Rights in America.* New York: Alfred A. Knopf, 1991.

Caldwell, Taylor. *The Arm and the Darkness.* New York: Aeonian Press, 1974.

Calhoun, John C. *The Papers of John Calhoun.* Edited by Robert L. Meriwether and Edwin Hemphill, Columbia, SC: University of South Carolina Press, 1959.

Carles, Emilie. *A Life of Her Own: A Country Woman in Twentieth Century France.* New Brunswick, NJ: Rutgers University Press, 1991.

Chatwin, Bruce. *Songlines.* New York: Penguin Books, 1988.

Churchill, Winston. *The Gathering Storm.* New York: Houghton Mifflin, 1948.

Clark, Kenneth. *Civilization.* New York: Harper & Row, 1970.

Cunningham, Noble E., ed. *Circular Letters of Congressmen to Their Constituents 1789-1829.* Chapel Hill: University of North Carolina Press, 1977.

Davis, Marilyn P. Davis. *Mexican Voices/American Dreams.* New York: Henry Holt & Co., 1991.

Dent, N.J.H. *Rousseau - An Introduction to His Psychological, Social, and Political Theory*. London: Basil Blackwell Ltd., 1988.

Dionne Jr., E. J. *Why Americans Hate Politics*. New York: Touchstone Book by Simon & Schuster, 1991.

"Survey of America," *The Economist* (26 October 1991).

"A Survey of China - When China Wakes," *The Economist*, (28 November 1992).

Fiske, John. *American Political Ideas Viewed from the Standpoint of Universal History*. New York, 1895. Irvine, CA: Reprint Services, Notable American Authors, 1992

Florinsky, Michael T. *Russia: A History and An Interpretation*. New York: Macmillan Co., 1958.

Fukuyama, Francis. *The End of History and the Last Man*. New York: The Free Press, 1992.

Gasset, Jóse Ortega y. *History as a System*. New York: W.W. Norton & Co., 1962.

Gay, Peter. *Voltaire's Politics: The Poet as Realist*. New Haven, : Yale University Press, 1988.

Geyl, Pieter. *Napolean For and Against*. London: Peregrine Paperbacks, 1949.

Glendon, Mary Ann. *Rights Talk - The Impoverishment of Political Discourse*. New York: The Free Press, 1991.

Halberstum, David. *The Next Century*. New York: William Morrow and Company, 1991.

Havel, Václav. *Disturbing the Peace - A Conversation with Karel Hvízdala*. Translated by Paul Wilson. New York: Vintage Books, 1990.

-------. *"Open Letters," Selected Writings 1965-1990*. Translated by Paul Wilson. New York: Vintage Books, 1991.

Hawking, Stephan W. *A Brief History of Time*. New York: Bantum Books, 1988.

Hawthorne, Nathaniel. *The American Presidency*. New York: Harcourt Brace, 1956.

Heinz, Hans-Joachim, and Lee, Marshall. *Namkwa - Life Among the Bushmen*. Boston: Houghton Mifflin Company, 1979.

Hobbes, Thomas. *Leviathan*. Edited by C. B. Macpherson, London: Penguin Books, 1985.

Hofstatder, Richard. *The American Political Tradition*. New York: Alfred A. Knopf, 1948.

Hourani, Albert. *A History of the Arab Peoples*. Cambridge, MA: The Belknap Press of the Harvard University Press, 1991.

Hume, David. *Dialogues Concerning Natural Religion*. New York: Harper Publishing Co., 1957.

Huntington, Samuel P. "The Clash of Civilizations," *Foreign Affairs* 72, no.3 (Summer 1993).

Jefferson, Thomas. *The Writings of Jefferson.* Edited by Merrill Peterson. New York: Library of America, 1984.

Johnson, Paul. *The Birth of the Modern; World Society 1815-1830.* New York: Harper Collins, 1991.

-------. *Modern Times.* New York: Harper Collins, 1991.

-------. *Intellectuals.* New York: Harper & Row, 1991.

Josephy Jr., Alvin M., ed. *America in 1492 the World of the Indian Peoples Before the Arrival of Columbus.* New York: Alfred Knopf, 1992.

Kaplin, Justin. *Lincoln Steffins.* New York: Simon & Schuster, 1974.

Kazernzadeh, Firuz. *The Struggle for Transcaucasia.* New York: The Philosophical Library, 1951.

Kennan, George. *Russia, the Atom and the West.* New York: Harper & Brothers, 1957.

-------. *Around the Cragged Hill.* New York: W.W. Norton & Company, 1993.

Kennedy, Paul. *The Rise and Fall of the Great Powers - Economic Change and Military Conflict from 1500-2000.* New York: Random House, 1987.

Kinross, Lord. *The Ottoman Centuries - The Rise and Fall of the Turkish Empire.* New York: Morrill Quill Paperbacks, 1977.

Klare, Michael. "The Next Great Arms Race," *Foreign Affairs* 72, no. 3 (Summer 1993).

Kohn, Hans. *The Idea of Nationalism - A Study of Its Origins and Background.* Toronto: Macmillan, 1967.

Kozol, Jonathan. *Savage Inequalities: Children in American Schools.* New York: Crown Publishers, 1991.

Larina, Anna. *This I Cannot Forget.* New York: W.W. Norton & Company, 1993.

Latourette, Kenneth Scott. *The Chinese.* London: Macmillan, 1956.

Lasch, Christopher. *The Culture of Narcissism.* New York: W.W. Norton & Company, 1979.

-------. *The True and Only Heaven - Progress and Its Critics.* New York: W.W. Norton & Company, 1991.

Locke, John. T*he Second Treatise on Government.* New York: Liberal Arts Press, 1952.

Lofton, Robert Jay. *The Protean Self: Human Resilience in the Age of Fragmentation.* New York: Basic Books, 1993.

Lowenberg, Bert James. *American History in American Thought.* New York: Simon & Schuster, 1972.

Machiavelli, Nicollò. *The Discourses.* Translated by Luigi Rizzi. New York: Carleton House, 1972.

-------. *The Prince.* New York: New American Library, 1952.

Markham, Beryl. *West With the Night.* Reprint of 1942 edition. New York: Landmark Books, 1985

Mayers, David. *George Kennan and the Dilemmas of U.S. Foreign Policy.* Oxford University Press, 1988.

McCoy, Drew R. *The Last of the Fathers - James Madison and the Republican Legacy.* Cambridge University Press, 1989.

Moss, Robert. *The War for the Cities.* New York: Coward, McCann & Geoghegan, Inc., 1972.

McDougall, Walter A. *Let the Sea Make a Noise...A History of the North Pacific from Magellan to MacArthur.* New York: Basic Books, 1994.

McKitrick, Eric., and Elkins, Stanley. *The Age of Federalism.* New York: Oxford University Press, 1993.

Menchú, Rigoberta. *I Rigoberta Menchú.* Edited by Elizabeth Burjos, translated by Ann Wright. London: Verso Press, 1984.

Mee Jr., Charles. *The Genius of the People.* Harper & Row, 1987.

Mill, John Stewart. *Utilitarianism, Liberty, and Representative Government.* New York: Everyman Library, 1950.

Milosz, Czeslaw. *The Captive Mind.* Vintage International Edition, 1990.

Morone, James A. *The Democratic Wish.* New York: Basic Books, 1990.

Mostert, Noël. *Frontiers - The Epic of South Africa's Creation and the Tragedy of the Xhosa Peoples.* New York: Alfred A. Knopf, 1992.

Murphy, Emmet C., with Snell, Michael. *The Genius of Sitting Bull: 13 Heroic Struggles for Business Leaders.* New York: Prentice Hall, 1952.

Netanyahu, Jonathan. *Self Portrait of a Hero.* New York: Ballantine Books, 1982.

Pangle, Thomas L. *Montesquie's Philosophy of Liberalism.* Chicago: University of Chicago Press, 1973.

Pipes, Richard. *The Russian Revolution.* New York: Vintage Books, 1991.

-------. *The Formation of the Soviet Union.* Cambridge, MA: Harvard University Press, 1957.

Ramazani, R.K. Revolutionary Iran. Baltimore, MD: John Hopkins University Press, 1986.

Raychandhur, H.C.R., and Majandhur, R.C., and Datta, K. *An Advanced History of India.* London: Macmillan & Co., 1958.

Reed, Stanley. "The Battle for Egypt," *Foreign Affairs* 72, no.4 (Sept/Oct 1993).

Rimini, Robert. *Andrew Jackson.* New York: Harper & Row, 1966.

Ripp, Victor. *Pizza in Pushkin Square.* New York: Simon & Schuster, 1992.

Rusk, Dean. *As I Saw It.* Penguin Books, 1990.

Russell, Bertrand. *A History of Western Philosophy.* New York: Simon & Schuster, 1945.

Safer, Morley. *Flashbacks on Returning to Vietnam.* Random House, 1990.

Schama, Simon. *Patriots and Liberators.* New York: Vintage Books, 1992.

-------. *Citizens: A Chronicle of the French Revolution.* New York: Alfred A. Knopf, 1989.

Sellars, Charles. *The Market Revolution.* New York: Oxford University Press, 1991.

Shklar, Judith N. *Montesquieu.* New York: Oxford University Press, 1987.

Smith, Robert J. Japanese Society. Cambridge University Press, 1983.

Spence, Jonathan. *The Search for Modern China.* New York: W.W. Norton, 1983.

Stavrianos, L.S. *The Promise of the Coming Dark Age.* San Francisco: W.H. Freeman and Company, 1976.

Stobbart, Lorraine. *Utopia Fact or Fiction? The Evidence From the Americas.* London: Allan Sutton Publishing, 1992.

Sutton, Peter., ed. *Dreamings: The Art of Aboriginal Australia.* New York: The Asia Society Gallery in New York in association with George Brazillier Publishers, 1988.

Terkel, Studs. *Race.* New York: New Press, 1992.

Tillich, Paul. *Love, Power, and Justice.* Cambridge, MA: Harvard University Press, 1954.

Toqueville, Alexis de. *Recollections of the French Revolution of 1848.* Edited by P. Mayer and A.P. Kerr. New Brunswick, New Jersey: Transaction Books, 1987.

-------. Democracy in America. New York: Vintage Books, 1958.

Tuchman, Barbara. *A Distant Mirror - The Calamitous 14th Century.* New York: Alfred A. Knopf, 1978.

Turner, Frederick Jackson. *The Frontier of American History.* Madison, WI: University of Wisconsin Press, 1921.

Wallace, William. *The Transformation of Western Europe.* London: Pinter, 1990.

Weaver, Richard. *Ideas Have Consequences.* Chicago: University of Chicago Press, 1948.

Wills, Gary., ed. *Lincoln at Gettysburg*. New York: Simon & Schuster, 1992.
Wilson, Woodrow. *A New Freedom*. New York, 1913.
Woodbridge, Frederick J.E. *The Purpose of History*. New York, 1916.

Index